A BETTER OFFERING

5 **Unmistakable Habits of Generous Churches**

DONALD A. SMITH
Foreword by J. Clif Christopher

To Amy, in celebration of our life together, and with gratitude to the Creator of the universe, who doesn't waste a single wilderness experience.

CONTENTS

FOREWORD

Over a decade ago, I wrote a book titled *Not Your Parents' Offering Plate* that challenged all the norms around Christian financial stewardship at that time. The bottom-line premise was that leaders within the Christian community—primarily the church—must make significant changes if they want to succeed in their mission of making disciples of Jesus Christ. Now, in this excellent new book, *A Better Offering: 5 Unmistakable Habits of Generous Churches*, Don Smith has taken seriously the challenge I gave years ago; only he's gone a step further by saying that the perfect time to implement radical change in church stewardship is *now*—not regardless of this world's post-pandemic state, but perhaps because of it.

The most powerful thing that comes across in Don's message is that making vital changes is not done just so the church can have the financial resources to survive current social, spiritual, and economic challenges, but so the church can more vibrantly fulfill its overall mission. This theme comes across throughout the pages as Don simply asks, "If we are not making disciples for Jesus and helping change the world, why keep doing it?"

For over a century, the church has passed the offering plate as a means to support itself, and over time, as the church has moved away from having a national tax, passing the plate has proved its worth. But not anymore. For the last fifty years, the church and the funds necessary for supporting it have been in decline. Money donated to religious entities continues to decrease as charitable gifts and new members coming into the faith are fewer and fewer. Change is demanded at every turn—we simply cannot stay the course and continue to watch the numbers disappear.

Don calls for a radical yet simple movement away from the passed plate toward a renewed discovery of generosity. This may well be one of the very foundations that a new church is built upon. That is why this book is much needed by today's clergy, laity, and anyone who not only wants the church to survive, but to thrive.

I have known Don for twenty-five years, and I have seen his work up close as he pastored several innovative and inspirational churches. I have heard him forcefully preach the gospel to eager congregations and watched him cry with a hurting member of his flock. His record in financial stewardship in each of his churches was magnificent, and the generosity of his people was exemplary. Over time, he transitioned into consulting, teaching, and training others to grow their skills and insights—the same people that led him to such success in making disciples. For the last fifteen years he has become a mentor to countless pastors and congregations while helping to bring new life in our changing times to the churches he has served. Now it is his turn to write his story so that even more people can learn from his vast experience.

Every pastor and financial leader of a congregation should read and study this book, then use it to move their people from contributing to committing.

J. Clif Christopher

YOU ARE HERE

IN THE MIDST OF THE UNIMAGINABLE

With only a canoe, a compass, and a map, Lewis and Clark set out on a journey from St. Louis, Missouri, to reach the base of the Rocky Mountains. It's where the map they held ended and their trek into unexplored land began. It was always assumed that the terrain in the West would be the same as in the East. It was not. Clearly, there were unexpected challenges ahead.

In his book, *Canoeing the Mountains: Christian Leadership in Uncharted Territory*, Tod Bolsinger writes:

> Lewis and Clark and the Corps of Discovery were about to go off the map and into uncharted territory. They would have to change plans, give up expectations, even reframe their entire mission. What lay before them was nothing like what was behind them. There were no experts, no maps, no "best practices" and no sure guides who could lead them safely and successfully. The true adventure—the real discovery—was just beginning.[1]

It was the summer of 2016 when I first read Bolsinger's book and felt blown away just thinking about the parallels of Lewis and Clark's predicament with the next phase of church leaders' journeys as they looked at the future and felt unequipped for the path before them. Now, looking back, I couldn't have imagined how life and ministry and church and leadership would change the way it did when COVID-19 entered the picture. Leadership books written years ago illustrate how leading the church pre-coronavirus was anxiety-producing enough, but they did not begin to prepare church leaders for navigating the mountainous, present-day changes they were facing in March 2020. The virus continues to this day to impact church life and every other aspect of living on the planet.

Lewis and Clark needed to give up
canoeing and embrace mountain climbing.

The seasons of pandemic and post-pandemic have been exhausting for church leaders, and if you're reading this, you are likely one of those leaders. In the midst of the unimaginable, I am honored that you would open this book, hoping to find some practical tools for your present and future ministry.

DROPPING SOMETHING IN
ORDER TO CLAIM YOUR FUTURE

I wonder if Lewis and Clark grieved the fact that they would have to leave behind their canoe—which had transported them all that way from St. Louis—in order to move forward over the mountains they faced. They knew, however, that in order to fulfill the purpose of their mission, they needed to leave behind the canoe that had brought them so far. Lewis and Clark needed to give up canoeing and embrace mountain climbing.

As a ministry strategist, coach, and mentor to pastors and church leaders, I am aware that one of the most difficult things for you to do is give up something that has served you well in order to embrace the new path God is calling you to take. I too have had to do the same. This book wasn't written in the flow of "normal" life as I knew it, but in a more isolated state during a pandemic—a season when most of the congregations and church leaders I work with have still not fully returned to in-person worship. Knowing that eventually the doors will reopen—albeit they don't know when—they are preparing for a post-pandemic time when mask-less people will again assemble within the church's walls. No one has the illusion that such a return will be as it was before.

One pastor, in a bi-weekly coaching conversation, stated:

> We are re-assessing everything. We believe that one of the benefits of this very difficult and painful season is that it gives us permission to literally look at everything we were doing before March 2020 happened and ask ourselves, "Do we need to continue to do that anymore, and if so, what will it need to look like now against the backdrop of our new reality?"[2]

Whew! Reassess *everything*? Now that's an ambitious strategy for ensuring that the future ministry and mission of the church align well with what church leaders believe God wants it to become.

There are several things, however, that I will invite you to reassess in the coming pages. As a generosity coach for pastors and church leaders, I will encourage you to consider how you've communicated and implemented your mission and ministry in the past and what might need to be left behind so you can embrace a new way of fully funding the work of God through your church. I will ask you to reassess how you invite people to financially invest in the mission of your church. In short, I will invite you to reassess how you help people discover the joy of generosity. I look forward to challenging you and your leaders to consider giving up some of the practices that have brought you this far but may not be needed for the journey ahead.

A WORD OF
ENCOURAGEMENT AND GRATITUDE

Over the past season, I have been reminded daily that different pastors and church leaders are reacting differently to the challenges being faced. Some are deeply assessing everything, and others are so overwhelmed that they feel paralyzed to even think beyond the planning of next week's worship experience.

Regardless of where you are in leading your congregation, let me simply say that not a day goes by that I am not moved and deeply inspired by all of the ways God is working through every leader I know. Each one has been gifted by the Spirit in differing ways. We have ongoing conversations about leading in whatever way necessary in order for their church to be whatever it can be for such a time as this. This equates to leaders getting creative and doing things they've never done before. It means leading in ways that go beyond their natural leadership propensities.

I've witnessed the fruit of this bold leadership each day of my ministry, especially on Sundays when I worship online with five to seven different churches each week. During these difficult times, I am inspired by the ways pastors and laypersons have boldly led like never before.

To you and to the other leaders in your church, I feel compelled to express how grateful I am to God for the ways God is using you in unexpected ways during these unimaginable times.

May the God who spoke through the prophet Ezekiel, a message of life and hope and restoration in the midst of a valley of dry bones, grant you that same hope today. And may the words of life in the midst of death give you the strength you need to continue to lead God's people into a new season with a new hope and a new vision. "I will put my Spirit in you and *you will live*... declares the Lord" (Ezekiel 37:14 NIV, emphasis added).

Grateful to be in ministry with you,
Donald A. Smith, MDiv

And now: the five unmistakable habits of generous churches—

HABIT 1:

SAY GOODBYE TO PASSING THE PLATES

START-UPS, TURNAROUNDS, AND A WILLINGNESS TO CHANGE

"Why would you want to start a church here? The timing isn't right." The seasoned pastor's words were, perhaps, the greatest gift I could have received just one month before moving to the suburbs to start a new church.

Shortly after that conversation, the first couple I visited about the new church told me after more than an hour-long conversation, "You can count on us. We'll do whatever it takes." Walking back to my car, I was a bit perplexed. They belonged to and were fully engaged in a five-thousand-member church in a nearby community. Now they were saying "whatever it takes" after hearing about a new church with no land, no building, and no members—no kidding! Even before my wife, Amy, and I moved into the heart of the community with our two children, we recruited twenty-five households in the area. After the move, one hundred cold calls a week for three consecutive weeks created a list of 117 households who were open to being on our contact list. Two months after our move, we had some worship experiences in different homes, then three months following our move, we had a celebratory preview service in a brand-new middle school with ninety-seven souls present.

When they discovered the opportunity
for a different kind of church from the one
in which they grew up, almost all of them
stuck around for the miracle to happen.

The following week, 225 people showed up for the launch, and the week after that, 175 attended worship. And that was the only time the attendance ever dipped below two hundred.

Over the next nine years, the church grew to 2,200 constituents and four weekend worship services averaging 1,300 children, youth, and adults.

Thinking back on that pastor's question, I'd say the time *was* right. Would you agree? And God sent the right people—generous people—who understood the importance of giving their whole selves for the work of God among us. By that, I mean they were people who brought with them the experiences, the expectations, and even the baggage of their past church communities in order to transform them into something new. So when they discovered the opportunity for a different kind of church from the one in which they grew up, almost all of them stuck around for the miracle to happen.

For more than twenty years, I was blessed to serve as lead pastor for five very different churches. They were

- a town and country church with only a few dozen members that was struggling to reach the community;

- a tiny country chapel with about four active families;
- a fifteen-year-old county seat church that was only one season away from closing its doors;
- a brand-new church in the suburbs; and
- a once-thriving church on a slow, steady, ten-year decline.

As I reflect on my pastoring years, my mind and heart are filled not only with amazement but with a deep sense of gratitude for the generous followers of Jesus with whom I had the privilege of being in ministry. Of this list, the new church in the suburbs was born in a big way, and the other four turnaround churches grew exponentially. Their leaders sensed that change was needed in order to reach more people, new people, and new kinds of people for Jesus.

They were vastly different congregations with varying circumstances, but one common attribute they all had was leaders who were willing to give up some old ways in order to create space for some new ones. In the wisdom of the writer of Ecclesiastes, each church faced the reality that there was "a time to plant and a time to uproot... a time to keep and a time to throw away" (Ecclesiastes 3:2, 6 NIV).

Most of today's churches face the same challenges and opportunities.

GIVING UP PLATE-PASSING FOR SOMETHING NEW

In his book *Necessary Endings*, Dr. Henry Cloud suggests that all of us will need to give up something in order to move forward. In life, this might be ending a business relationship, a personal relationship, or giving up a possession. In giving up something, space is then created for the birth of something new.[3]

For organizations—especially established ones—the necessary ending may be with an employee or a habit that is no longer effective.

Often, organizations such as churches need to give up a particular practice. This practice could be relatively new in its implementation but never gained enough traction to be fruitful or viable. After all, sometimes even new practices are hard to give up when hurt feelings are involved. In many instances, the practice is a longstanding tradition to which the leaders and people have become accustomed, and passing the offering plate is one of those long-established practices. Even with some diminished use of plate-passing, which was designed for the cash-and-check-payment era, it continues to this day in most churches.

> You may just need to give up some long-held
> practices in order to up your giving.

Now I will examine the possibilities for the future as practices such as plate-passing are ended in order to create space for new, refreshing, and life-giving opportunities for generosity to happen. In other words, you may just need to give up some long-held practices in order to up your giving.

FORMER PASTOR AND FORMER PLATE-PASSING ADVOCATE

Confession: I used to be one who *insisted* that the plate be passed during worship. As a former pastor, plate-passing was a part of the weekly rhythm of churches I served. In the 1980s, when the "edgy" new congregations began placing contribution boxes at the entrances/exits of the worship center, I thought they had lost their minds.

In the mid-1990s, when I was assigned as founding pastor to plant a new church, we launched worship in a brand-new middle school, and for our first worship service ever in the cafetorium, we were prepared for the offering time. Already purchased from the church resource catalogue were four, new, shiny brass plates, each with a deep red felt bottom and a gold, orthodox cross embroidered into the felt disk. The plates were given by a family on the launch team as a special part of a "wish list" campaign for items needed for the launch. Twenty-five years later, I'm guessing that those plates are still being passed along with the other four matching plates that were purchased when we moved out of the school and into the newly constructed facility.

In my post-pastor years, I began coaching, mentoring, and training new church start pastors. The influence of the edgy churches was beginning to have an effect on the church planter mentality. I had a typical narrative that I used during the training for stewardship and finances: "Pass the plates—or baskets—during worship. Do it as an act of worship. Invite people to consider the joy of generosity by passing the plates among those gathered for worship." Dismissing the box-in-the-back-of-the-room strategy, I would add, "Do not rob the people in your new church of the opportunity to discover the joy of generosity." Strong words, indeed!

A DIFFERENT WORLD–
A NEW OPPORTUNITY

Through the years, as I continued to work with churches all over the country, I'm happy to say that I softened a bit. Now, as e-giving has slowly become part of the generosity culture of the church, the passing of the plate has continued in most churches. Why? I suppose that, for most, it's one of many "because we've always done it that way" practices. And to be clear, the preferred method of giving for many households is still to bring a check or an envelope with a contribution and to place it in the offering receptacle that is passed during worship.

Ben Stroup of Velocity Strategy Solutions helps organizations navigate the ever-changing global marketplace. Ben loves to ask the question, "Shouldn't we be renegotiating all of our cultural permission systems?" This is because, through the decades, we have been reminded that "every cultural reality that was supposed to be true was no longer true. Every single time it was supposed to be predictable, it changed." Most recently, the systems that we associated with church have definitely changed. Think about these changes: how we attend church, what time we go to church, how we support the church, how we connect in small groups, how we define the mission field of our church. Stroup states, "Now we can connect with the church anytime, anyplace, and on any device. And you can still stay plugged in to your home church and listen to preachers from all over the world. So much that was predictable prior to COVID is gone."[4]

> Many believe that the days of "receiving the offering" by ushers passing a receptacle are long past.

All of this is due to unforeseen realities which have happened and will continue to happen in the future. And when such a season happens, there is change in the marketplace (and, for our purposes, that marketplace is the world in which we have been called to be the church). The response for some leaders is to charge the hill with a sense of awareness and urgency. Other leaders will sit in a corner. "Either we become mobilized or paralyzed," Stroup believes, "and there is no middle ground."[5]

Related to this discussion, the offering plate becomes a metaphor. Perhaps passing the plate represents something that has become predictable, even though the world has drastically changed since plate-passing was first implemented. Do we continue to do something with the mindset of "It's just what we do," or do we renegotiate this and other aspects of the church's systems and procedures?

After all, many believe (myself included) that the days of "receiving the offering" by ushers passing a receptacle are long past. More than that, the mere act of passing a plate or a basket during worship in the twenty-first century may be one of the most bewildering parts of the worship experience. Why? Because in most churches across America, the plates or baskets are still very empty at the end of the offering time, which creates an awkward and tangible reminder that people aren't giving. The message it sends to first-time guests and even members is confusing, and church leaders should be troubled by this trend.

Yet the prospect of *no longer* passing the plate is anxiety-producing for some. How do I know? If you want to find out how important a certain practice is to a person or to an organization, just take it away—and that's exactly what happened to every single congregation in America in March of 2020.

COVID-19 is a dreadful virus that, at the time of this book-writing, had infected more than 57 million people worldwide. As I complete the manuscript for this book, more than 1.4 million people across the globe have died, with more than 300,000 of those Americans.

In my life as a ministry strategist, I have had an "in the trenches" view of the amazing work that God does through the church. For as long as I can remember, Romans 8:28 has been meaningful to me: "And we know that in all things God works for the good of those who love [God]" (NIV). Even when something horrific happens, good comes out of it, and God, working through people and organizations, shows up in amazing—sometimes miraculous—ways. One way I have sensed God bringing good out of the bad during the pandemic is how God's Spirit is inspiring church leaders across the country in new, creative, visionary ways. For many, this season has become an opportunity to evaluate and/or revisit just about every ministry, every mission, and every practice. This is especially true regarding worship in that it has continued but in ways we never imagined. And one of the questions that leaders have asked is, "How do we invite people to give if we can't pass the plates now nor in the foreseeable future, even after we come back to in-person worship?"

Let me say clearly that passing the offering plate is not a major priority when viewed against the backdrop of a pandemic. But in the hundreds of conversations I've had with church leaders since March 2020, finance teams and committees all over the country are wondering about the answer to this question: *When can we get back to that part of worship when we pass the plates?*

One answer is, *you don't have to.* You really don't have to physically pass the plate ever again. Are you having a hard time grasping that emotionally or practically or spiritually? Before you reject the idea, at least have a conversation with yourself and fellow leaders about it and invite God's Spirit to be present in the process.

Only 46 percent of congregations offer online giving. Just let that sink in.

Months after in-person worship ceased because of COVID-19, Lake Institute on Faith and Giving surveyed 1,200 congregations of varying sizes across the United States. Of these congregations, only 12 percent stated that they were teaching on financial generosity at least once a month. Of that 12 percent, 73 percent reported *increased* revenue in spite of the absence of in-person gatherings.

David King, president of Lake Institute, emphasizes that, for most congregations, contributions given during in-person worship are still a source of 78 percent of revenue. And only 46 percent of congregations offer online giving. Just let that sink in. In the twenty-first century, more than half of all congregations rely solely on receiving contributions by mail or people bringing their tithes and offerings to the church. In a COVID-19 world and beyond, this is not a sustainable strategy.

Even more important than how people give, King emphasizes the *why* of people's generosity: "The pandemic just raised the stakes."[6]

THE TEMPLE OFFERING, THE EARLY CHURCH, AND THE POST-PANDEMIC CHURCH

Since visiting the Holy Land for the first time in 1992, I have been fascinated by the view from the Mount of Olives looking west across the Kidron Valley toward the Temple Mount. The Temple Mount is the massive enclosure where the Jerusalem Temple once stood. Approximately thirty-seven acres in size today, the Temple Mount is more than five hundred yards long by 350 yards wide. The Israel Museum, Jerusalem, has a first-century scaled model of Jerusalem that helps connect the dots showing where the Second Temple, a.k.a. Herod's Temple, may have been located within that enclosure. Illustrations of this temple reveal an interior courtyard named Court of the Women. Scholars believe that this courtyard would have been the setting for the widow's offering story in Luke:

> He looked up and saw rich people putting their gifts into the treasury; he also saw a poor widow put in two small copper coins. He said, "Truly I tell you, this poor widow has put in more than all of them; for all of them have contributed out of their abundance, but she out of her poverty has put in all she had to live on" (Luke 21:1–4 NRSV).

A study of the text suggests that, while observing the happenings that day in the courtyard, Jesus may have been seated on the steps that led up to the Holy of Holies, or the inner sanctuary of the Tabernacle. This appears to be the only place where Jesus and his disciples would have had a clear view of the temple treasury. The temple offerings were brought to the courtyard and placed in one or many of the thirteen trumpet-shaped copper receptacles. Six of the receptacles were for required offerings, and the remaining seven were for freewill offerings.[7]

Some points for consideration:

- **Coins being thrown into trumpet-shaped copper receptacles would have been noisy!** If someone wanted others to *hear* how generous they were, they would simply forcefully throw in many coins. Jesus, of course, was not impressed with this. In the Sermon on the Mount, he warned, "When you give to the needy, do not announce it with trumpets, as the hypocrites do" (Matthew 6:2 NIV).

- **The causes needing support were many.** Each receptacle represented a cause. Some were of communal importance, and all people were instructed to support them. Other causes appealed to the donor's particular passion.

- **People *brought* their offerings to the temple and then to the receptacles within the temple.** The receptacles were not passed among the people.

Our spiritual DNA suggests that offerings are to be brought, not taken; presented, not collected.

Not long after this teaching moment with Jesus, the early church gathered post-resurrection to live out the commission to go into the world. Part of preparing for this bold, global movement meant the people gathered together and shared everything they had. During part of these communal gathering times, they would place their resources before the apostles.

> The whole group of those who believed were of one heart and soul, and no one claimed private ownership of any possessions, but everything they owned was held in common. With great power the apostles gave their testimony to the resurrection of the Lord Jesus, and great grace was upon them all. There was not a needy person among them, for as many as owned lands or houses sold them and brought the proceeds of what was sold. They laid it at the apostles' feet, and it was distributed to each as any had need (Acts 4:32–35 NRSV).

Once again, the people of God in the early church *brought* their offerings. For the early followers of Jesus, this meant bringing everything to the gatherings and presenting their gifts to God by laying them at the feet of the apostles.

Early in ministry, I was friends with the pastor of a predominantly Black church in town. One day, we met at her church so I could tour the facility. While in the sanctuary, we discussed the very different ways that our respective congregations observed the offering time. For our church, the baskets were passed. This practice was referred to as "receiving the offering" with the oft-spoken words, "As the ushers come forward to receive the offering." Sometimes, it was called "taking the offering." For her congregation, however, the invitation was very different: "This morning, we have come to God's house with our gifts. At this time, bring your gifts to God." Following the invitation, as music played, people would bring their gifts forward to the plates located at the chancel/stage area. Two *very* different offering experiences!

According to the passages I mentioned in Luke and Acts, our spiritual DNA suggests that offerings are to be brought, not taken; presented, not collected. Offering containers are stationary—like the copper trumpets—not passed. There is precedent for a set-aside time for offering gifts, but our faith heritage suggests that passing a container among the people does not align with the formational stories of bringing gifts to God.

A BRIEF HISTORY OF PLATE-PASSING

In a position paper by David C. Norrington, "Fund-raising: The methods used in the Early Church compared with those used in English Churches Today," he goes into great detail about many modern practices that have little or no origin in scripture. Instead, they've emerged in the post-apostolic church, sometimes hundreds of years after the time of Jesus.

Norrington notes that, during the public ministry of Jesus, nowhere do we hear him make an appeal for contributions or alms, though his parables do teach on the stewardship of resources. According to his instructions to the disciples in Matthew 10:9, he said not to accept alms. Jesus seems to have graciously received gifts of hospitality, which was a typical custom for a teacher as a guest in someone's home. Through the love of his followers, the needs of Jesus were cared for.

If the ministry of Jesus did not significantly shape the financial practices of the modern church, the urging of Apostle Paul for Christians to be generous certainly did. Paul encouraged churches, almost in a competitive way, to give generously. Such examples were the Corinthian and Macedonian churches (see 2 Corinthians 8:1–7), and particularly the appeal of all churches to support the impoverished Jerusalem church (see Acts 11:27–30). Paul received gifts for travel assistance (see 1 Corinthians 16:6) and mission support (see Philippians 4:16). [8]

With the Acts 2 church, the people of The Way not only brought gifts, they brought *all* of their possessions and placed them at the feet of the apostles. These resources were freely shared among the group of Jesus followers that had grown from 120 in number to over ten thousand in a short period of time. As these resources were generously offered, the contributions were then distributed to those who had need. In short, gifts were brought and not taken.

So, if our biblical heritage does not establish a foundation for passing an offering container, when did it start?

In 2008, Frank Viola and George Barna released a book, *Pagan*

Christianity, that made quite a stir. Tracing many of the modern-day Christian practices back to pagan cultures, the book illustrates the ways that many items and practices in the modern church (candles, clergy vestments, celebrating high holy days such as Easter, creating and building specific church architecture and furnishings, etc.) came from pagan origins. Yes, one of these influences on modern-day Christianity was the "alms dish"—an offering plate that did not appear in Christian practices until post-Reformation sixteenth-century, but can be traced, along with many other practices in the modern church, back to the Jewish and Greco-Roman worlds from fourth-century BC to fourth-century AD.[9]

Through their research, Viola and Barna remind us that ushers didn't originate until the sixteenth century. During the reign of Elizabeth I, the liturgy of the Church of England was reorganized, and the role of usher was created. As stated in an email to Viola from Professor John McGuckin in 2002, the term *usher* would have come from the Anglo-Saxon word for "a person who guides people into court or church." Ushers had many responsibilities, including recording who took communion, escorting people to their assigned seat, and yes, collecting the offering.

In 2009, *Christianity Today* looked into the history of plate-passing in the American church in an article by Mark Rogers fittingly titled, *Passing the Plate.* Based on Rogers's research, not until the early 1800s did this practice commence in America. In the colonies, the church was originally government sanctioned and government funded. Following the American Revolution, however, the colonies continued to establish and fund the Congregational and Anglican churches in their particular communities. Rogers observed, "Most of the colonies could not imagine states without an established church." Churches, therefore, even in the early decades of America, were funded by taxes and fees, like property and poll taxes—but not through voluntary offerings.

Not until 1833, when Massachusetts rescinded its religious tax, did every state in the union dis-establish its churches. Church leaders now had to find new ways to raise funds in order to survive and thrive in the free-market religion of the nineteenth century. This included pew taxes (yes, you had to pay extra to sit up front!), writing a "pledge" in a publicly distributed book, and passing a container among the people that, for most churches, became an offering plate.

Rogers goes on to advocate for the practice of passing the plate. In asking the question, "What's the point of doing this in the modern world?" he then goes on to say that having people grasp a plate during worship reminds them that (like the early church) everything they possess ultimately belongs to God.[10]

At one time in my ministry, I would have agreed with Rogers's conclusion. I even would have agreed if asked about this matter five years ago. *In today's modern world, I believe that passing an offering receptacle during worship is a practice that no longer represents the depth and breadth of the offering.* It no longer symbolizes the full means through which God's people are being inspired to generously bring their gifts—gifts that will be distributed in ways that impact the whole world for the better.

What has become the highly revered, ceremonial passing of the offering plate is a practice that is actually less than one hundred years old.

The Rev. Dr. L. Edward Phillips, associate professor at Candler School of Theology, reviewed the history of the offering in the Methodist movement. Initially, the word *offering* was associated with the Eucharist (Holy Communion) and referred to as the dedication of the whole person (including monetary gifts) as an offering to the Creator.

By 1920, giving during the Methodist service was referred to as "the collection," and by the 1930s, the collection of monetary contributions was referred to as "the offering." Eventually, a standard rhythm for an offering then developed, with ushers reverently coming forward to receive the plates for collecting the money. The offering time was accompanied by a song (instrumental or vocal), followed by the rising of the people in song (Doxology), followed by a prayer of dedication for the offerings received.[11]

In regard to the word *offering*, it is interesting to me that what was originally intended to mean the dedication of the whole self for the work of God, evolved in only a matter of decades into a reverent practice of offering monetary gifts to support the work of God. And what has become the highly revered, ceremonial passing of the offering plate is a practice that is actually less than one hundred years old.

A NEW SEASON, A NEW CONVERSATION

Given this relevant background, I am now inviting church leaders to at least have a conversation and rethink the offering time; better yet, say *goodbye* to passing the plates or any other containers. And let me clarify, this doesn't mean eliminating the offering time altogether, just eliminating the practice of passing a container. Perhaps now you're wondering, *if we don't pass plates, then what shall we do and for what purpose will we do it?* That's a great question, and it should lead to productive conversations among the leaders of your church. Bottom line, the time for rethinking the offering is now.

Think about it. Beginning in March of 2020, in only a matter of weeks,

- most of us thought about *attending church* differently;

- most of us thought about *doing small groups* differently;

- most of us thought about *church meetings* differently;

- most of us realized that *our mission* was bigger than we ever imagined and that *our mission field* was much bigger than our geographic location;

- most of us had to rethink our ministries of *hospitality and prayer*;

- most of us thought about *one-time* and *recurring e-giving* differently; and

- I'm guessing *all* of us began to think about *the offering* differently.

Yes, *all* of us who were passing a container in worship in February 2020 stopped doing so by March, and out of necessity, we began to think differently about the offering.

Going back to early American Christianity, it's amazing to me that, until 1833, our churches were funded by the colonies and the states. Therefore, after independence was declared in 1776, it took almost sixty years to move past the DNA of the church-and-state arrangement in Britain. During these decades, many churches, fully funded by the state, may not have had an offering time during worship. Then entered the frontier expressions of Christianity, such as Methodism, which came to America yearning for a new beginning for a church that was *not* state sponsored.

John Wesley, who founded the Methodist movement in England in the mid-1700s, spoke prophetically about financial generosity. In one of the most impactful sermons of his ministry, *The Use of Money*, Wesley spoke of three rules, the third being, "Give all you can." As he witnessed the growth and the challenges of the movement, he became increasingly concerned about the British Methodists and the American movement that was experiencing exponential growth. In 1789, Wesley referenced his sermon on money, which had been printed in 1759, and he lamented:

Of the three rules which are laid down… you may find many that observe the first rule, namely, gain all you can. You may find a few that observe the second, save all you can. But how many have you found that observe the third rule of give all you can? Have you reason to believe that five hundred of these are to be found among fifty thousand Methodists? [12]

As different generations addressed Christian stewardship in various ways, the offering eventually became a part of the worship life of congregations in America. Until 2020, most of those churches passed some kind of container among those gathered for worship at some point during the service.

As this book is being written, many congregations in America are still not conducting in-person worship. And for those that are back in person in some limited capacity, the plate is still not being passed because of pandemic-related protocols. As noted earlier, a majority of those congregations that were already intentionally addressing financial generosity at least monthly prior to COVID-19 are not experiencing a negative impact on giving. To the contrary, they are thriving financially during the pandemic. They are doing this without in-person worship and without a physical container being passed among the worship attenders.

Instead of saying, "We've never done it that way before," let us say, "We never have to do it that way again!"

How can churches thrive financially without in-person worship? Many, if not all of us, were asking this question. Since then, some churches have exceeded their previous year's contributions during a season of virtual life together. Others are on track, thanks to funding assistance from outside sources. Still others have struggled mightily. But every church has had to reassess the means through which the offering time has been implemented and contributions have been received.

Even though church life has drastically changed, I am reminded that the principles of generosity have not. Through modifying the mechanism of how people are "bringing" the offering—without concern that "we've never done it this way before"—churches that have thrived have found a way to communicate and create a virtual environment for generosity to happen. They've done this by remembering:

- Everything we possess ultimately belongs to the One from whom our blessings have been given.

- Our heartfelt response to the Creator for these blessings is one of gratitude and generosity.

- How we steward our resources is important to God. Remember, Jesus taught, "Where your treasure is, there will your heart be also" (Matthew 6:21 NIV). Or, my favorite translation is from *The Message*, "It's obvious, isn't it? The place where your treasure is, is the place you will most want to be, and end up being."

- During worship, we should set aside a time to meditate on the call to live a generous life and to offer our *whole selves* to God.

- During worship, we should celebrate the work of God that happens through our collective generosity.

- Worship can happen any time and any place!

Through a season of pandemic, an offering brought by God's people without physical plates or ushers in brick and mortar sanctuaries has resulted in an unexpected season of financial generosity. So instead of saying, "We've never done it that way before," let us say, "We never have to do it that way again!" We don't need to circulate a receptacle every weekend, fifty-two times a year, but what *will* this practice look like in the future? How will we invite God's people to support God's work in our midst and into the world?

A PASTOR, A NEW CHURCH, AND A NEW WAY OF THINKING

In 2016, a new church was born. With its new beginning, the founding pastor, Travis Garner, and leaders were able to design everything from the ground up, especially the worship experience. As a fundraising strategist for this congregation, I have been inspired from the moment we became partners in ministry. In a conversation with the pastor, we discussed the thinking behind the decisions that were made leading up to the birth of the church. The following reflects this church's journey that, hopefully, will inspire other churches for inviting people to live generously.

Pastor Travis Garner shared:

> We knew from the beginning that we weren't going to pass a container because we wanted financial giving to be only one of many ways people could respond to the message of the day. The entire worship experience—whether in the middle school or virtually—is designed for people to be able to participate in various ways. Following each message, people are invited to move toward one of the stations where communion is served. As people receive the Sacrament, there are other ways they might respond, such as
>
> • pray at one of the kneeling places provided or back at their seat;
>
> • receive prayer and support from those who are stationed to do so;

- speak to a church leader a desire to make a decision for Christ or be baptized or join the church; or

- go to one of the six baskets scattered throughout the worship space to bring an offering.

We wanted to create more than just a perfunctory "walk down the aisle if you want to join the church" invitation. People are encouraged to do whatever they feel compelled to do in response to God's leading.[13]

So, during its brief four-year history, *this church has* never *passed a container among the people.* Baskets are still available in the worship space, but like many other churches over the past four years, the offerings placed there continue to decrease.

Here are some interesting statistics for this particular church. Remember, this congregation started in 2016:

Year	Percent of Annual Income Received in Baskets	Percent of Annual Income Received Online	Percent of Annual Income Received Through Other (text-to-give, checks received other than on Sunday, prepaid, stock, etc.)
Year 1	48%	42%	10%
Year 2	38.5%	51%	10.5%
Year 3	27%	61%	12%
YTD Year 4 (pandemic)	5.3%	82%	11.7%

As you can see, prior to the pandemic, this church was already receiving a large percentage of income through "virtual baskets" that were available 24/7/365. And when in-person worship ceased, giving naturally continued. Through July 2020, the church was ahead of the previous year's income even as expenses were significantly reduced when in-person worship at the school stopped and virtual worship for all began.

Over the past months, I continue to hear lamentation from church leaders because "we aren't able to pass the plates like we used to." I also hear words of hope and confidence that "when in-person worship returns, we never have to pass the plate again."

It's a new season and a time to rethink the offering.

There could be a different way—a better way.

CONVERSATION STARTERS FOR YOUR TEAM

1. In a sentence or two, describe the theology of stewardship and generosity in your church.

2. Review the history and current practices for the offering in your faith community. How does this reflect your church's theology of stewardship and generosity?

3. As you consider not including the passing of a container, what feelings come to the surface?

HABIT 2

SAY HELLO TO STORYTELLING

JESUS TOLD STORIES, AND WE CAN TOO!

Mark 4:33–34 conveys the importance of storytelling in the ministry of Jesus by saying, "With many stories like these, he presented his message to them, fitting the stories to their experience and maturity. He was never without a story when he spoke" (MSG). This leads me to ask that if we were to say goodbye to plate-passing, how can the offering time be repurposed in a new, refreshing, and inspiring way? Well, according to Mark, Jesus didn't speak to the people without stories, so why shouldn't we.

I think it's safe to say that every church has a host of modern-day stories of how God is working among the people through their particular ministries, so doesn't it make sense to tell at least one of those stories every week? As we bid farewell to the passing of the plate, let's look at replacing it with intentional storytelling the way Jesus did.

IT'S REALLY NOT YOUR
PARENTS' OFFERING PLATE

Even when a good and trusted friend tells you how to inspire greater giving in a very different yet simple way, it can still be hard to believe that their seemingly wise counsel will actually work. This scenario describes my journey as a pastor.

My friend and colleague, Dr. J. Clif Christopher, founder and president of Horizons Stewardship, wrote a book in 2008 called *Not Your Parents' Offering Plate*. This book has become, for many pastors, leaders, and finance teams, a basic handbook for growing financial generosity in the church. Dr. Christopher provides details for a simple strategy of Sunday morning storytelling immediately prior to the offering. In one or two minutes, the person making the pre-offering appeal *replaces* the verbiage typically used before an offering with a life-changing story.

For example, a normal offering script goes like this: "God has been so good and has showered us with blessings far more abundantly than we could have imagined. As a response to God's goodness, let us now prepare our hearts to give back to God a portion of the blessings we've been given. The ushers will now come forward to receive our tithes and offerings." Then there is silence as the ushers make their way down the aisle and the plates are handed off—possibly followed by a prayer—and as the plates are passed, music is played or a song is sung. Then, depending on each particular Christian expression, the offering is followed by the Doxology or other appropriate post-offering song as the plates are taken to a counting room. Of course, each church's ritual will vary, but they all have the commonality of five to ten minutes of time.

In his book, Dr. Christopher suggests something more like this:

> Do not give an invitation for the ushers to come forward. They already know when to come down the aisle, so it's not necessary—they simply start walking when the story begins. The person sharing that week might say, "Wow,

friends, this past week was amazing! Ninety-six volunteers and 225 children packed the worship center as well as every available classroom for our annual Vacation Bible Camp (VBC). Fifty of the children were not previously connected to our church, and at least one of them had never been told about the love of Jesus… until this week! On the last day, the father of that child said to the teacher, 'Thank you so much for teaching our daughter about Jesus. We've never felt like we could do it, and we're so happy that she, and all of our family, have found a safe place to learn more about God. By the way, we can't stop singing the songs together!' With permission to share this conversation from that little girl's grateful dad, I just want to say to each one of you this morning, *thank you* for your generosity. We offer VBC for *free* to any child, and we're able to do that because of *you*. In this case, your generosity made a difference in a little girl's life *and* her family's. Thank you for investing in VBC and every life-changing ministry with children at our church."

Then, per Dr. Christopher's instructions, the ushers should start passing the plates when the story ends (remember, this book was written when many church leaders were assuming that plate-passing was a given).

Christopher's conclusion in 2008:

> The time it takes to tell the story and receive the offering should be the same amount of time as the conventional way, and the story being shared should change every week. Do this over a fifty-two-week period every year, and the donors of the church get an ongoing narrative to connect the offering with the changed lives, all made possible through the collective generosity of the people.[14]

This suggested new practice sounded like a good idea the first time I heard him speak about it, but I wondered if it would actually work.

So, in the last church that I pastored, I decided to implement this "life-changing story" strategy. The staff and leaders were fully committed to creating the stories and implementing the plan we created—and the leaders of the church and I were blown away by the results. Over a three-year period, financial generosity supporting the ongoing ministries of the church grew by 33 percent for an increase of $1 million in annual contributions.

> Today, we need to say it even more emphatically: it's *really not* our parents' offering plate! It's a virtual plate that doesn't need to be passed in a physical way.

I'm so grateful for the impact Clif Christopher's visionary leadership has had in my life—and many others'—during the past thirty years. Now, I believe it's time more than ever to revisit his storytelling strategy described above. Why? Because we are reminded that traditional plate-passing, as a practice, has run its course of efficacy. In the modern church, the metaphor of the offering plate continues to change. Fifteen years ago, the mindset was that it's not our parents' offering plate. Today, we need to say it even more emphatically: it's *really not* our parents' offering plate! It's a virtual plate that doesn't need to be passed in a physical way. Changing this part of worship allows for even greater focus on the stories of God working in and through us and the many ways that we can be inspired to generously and gratefully respond to those stories.

What would happen if the offering time focused on the stories pointing to a virtual realm of giving opportunities, *in lieu of* passing a physical plate? Instead of focusing on the choreography of people passing a physical container, why not focus on the stories that celebrate the work of God in our midst, and invite people to invest in that work through a number of virtual or physical ways? This makes the offering time more about the life-changing work of the Spirit through the congregation. If we tell the stories well, then people will understand what's at stake. And if they understand where the money is being invested—and if they believe that God's Spirit is in the midst of that work—then generosity will follow.

It's all about the stories—one changed life at a time—and the Creator of the universe who brings those stories to life.

OPPORTUNITIES LOST

As much as Clif Christopher's life-changing story counsel has worked for me and so many others, it surprises me that a vast majority of the churches I have attended over the years still do not utilize this concept as a way to celebrate the good work that God is doing all week every week, all year every year!

As non-profit entities, congregations have an advantage that very few charitable organizations have: their people gather at least once a week! Even during the pandemic and post-pandemic season, churches continued to gather, only online. The buildings were closed and locked, but the churches stayed open; in-person worship stopped, but worship itself never wavered. And of course, the God who called each of those churches into being continued to work in and through each congregation, only in new ways. The weekly gathering of people is a key part to a congregation's life in community. How many other non-profits would *love* to gather with a good portion of their donors at least once a week? They *all* would!

Sadly, however, only a small percentage of congregations utilize the weekly gathering as an opportunity to tell the stories of God's work in their midst. As a whole, the church has failed to communicate the true and inspiring accounts of life change. In doing so, the church has failed to communicate how donations are being invested and the impact that giving is making. Because of that, donors have become confused and even disheartened about how their contributions are being stewarded. And because of that, donors are finding other organizations to support and redirecting their giving to other charitable causes.

For the past forty years, statistics illustrate the slow, definitive decline in giving to religious non-profits—churches are now receiving an ever-shrinking piece of the charitable pie. The "Giving USA 2020" annual report from The Giving Institute illustrates this decline, and the numbers are alarming. Since 1956, the institute has been providing this report on charitable giving in America, and one that the strategists in our organization receive each year. The report offers data regarding sources, recipients of charitable gifts, and the trends reflected in these statistics.

The report (which reflects charitable giving in 2019) reveals the continuing decline of giving to religion. To be clear, Americans give 1.9 percent of their disposable income (after taxes) to charitable causes. In 2019, the total amount that individuals gave to 501(c)(3) non-profits grew to $449.64 billion, and religious causes received 29 percent of every dollar given. Yes, religion is America's favorite charity! Education is a distant second at 17 percent. So, what's the problem? The problem is that, in 1980, the annual report indicated that religion received more than 59 percent of every charitable dollar given. So, in forty years, religion's share of American charitable giving has declined by more than 50 percent.[15]

These statistics are staggering, especially for me and for others who continue to direct most, if not all, of our household charitable contributions to religious causes. What is the reason for this shift in donor-directed dollars? Why is the church losing ground in the non-profit charitable realm?

While writing this book, I did a little digging. On a whim, I googled Heart Association, and of course, the first site that popped up was the

American Heart Association. *Wow!* The entire home page was designed to connect me to the cause, to the stories, and to a person who, if needed, could chat with me *at that very minute* about the life-changing, life-saving work of the organization! There were six different links on the page where I was invited to click and give. By contrast, on many church websites, it's difficult to even find a Give or Donate button to click.

When I went on a regional Habitat for Humanity homepage, within thirty seconds I was able to read the two-sentence summaries of the compelling stories of Barbara, Ronessa, and Samantha. Another click took me to the full version of these three inspiring stories with the message: Do you want to invest in making more of this happen? *Together We Build.*

You may want to do some digging as well. Non-profits are not shy about asking people to invest generously, and they love to tell the miraculous stories that happen through the generosity of their donors. The church, however, seems to shy away from "the ask"—also known as "the invitation to give." Individual congregations and their leaders just don't seem that interested in investing the time and resources needed to tell the stories that will inspire generous giving.

As you consider making changes with the hope and expectation of getting different results from the past, please keep these three things in mind:

1. **The philanthropic marketplace is more competitive than ever.** In 2011, the IRS reported that there were 1.1 million non-profit organizations in America. By 2018 (the most recent data available), that number had grown to more than 1.3 million.

2. **Fundraising practices for institutional non-profits continue to grow and evolve as the world changes.** Most churches, however, use the same tactics that were working for them decades ago.

3. **Institutional non-profits have perfected the art of story-telling.** Lives are being changed, and their donors are given consistent reminders of how the money is being stewarded by the organization. Churches, on the other hand, seem to assume that people know what's happening, so they don't need to tell the stories to their donors. Or they may have come to expect that people are going to give to the church because they're supposed to give to the church.

The reality is that non-profit fundraising will continue to become even more highly competitive. Statistics are clear that religious organizations are falling behind in doing what it takes to compete in the twenty-first century philanthropic marketplace. As leaders in this new reality, it may be time for you to consider a new strategy for a new day.

A RESOURCE FOR CREATING A CULTURE OF STORYTELLING IN WORSHIP

Charitable organizations like the American Heart Association and Habitat for Humanity don't have a corner on the market for stories of changed lives. Typically, however, they just do a better job telling their stories. It doesn't have to be that way.

This illustrates a simple formula for generosity:
Understanding + Ownership + Inspiration = Generosity!

As an added resource for church leaders, I've created *The How-To Guide for Storytelling in Worship.* An introduction to the guide, including a link to this complimentary resource, can be found in the final section of this book. It provides a more detailed, step-by-step process for creating an indigenous storytelling strategy for your particular congregation. God is working 24/7/365 through the ministries of your church to change lives for the better. It's important that we create space for sharing those stories.

And when church leaders are able to take *The How-To Guide* and apply it to their context, it's a joy to hear the stories that are told and the fruitfulness of the result. It's exciting to see how people respond once they comprehend *(understanding)* more clearly how the leaders of the church are investing the donor dollars well, and with tangible, life-changing results. When people understand it, feel a part of it *(ownership)*, and believe that God is in the midst of it *(inspiration)*, then generosity happens. This illustrates a simple formula for generosity:

Understanding + Ownership + Inspiration = Generosity!

Many churches are *thriving* in the midst of some of the most economically uncertain times that we've experienced. Currently, they are not passing any kind of physical offering container for their weekend services, mainly because many churches haven't returned to in-person worship. Understandably, the ones that are opening back up aren't going to be passing containers among the people for a very long time, if ever. And yet, many of these churches are above year-to-date projected giving and ahead of year-over-year giving compared to 2019.

There are many things that these congregations do well, but telling the story of real lives changed by God through real ministry and mission is a common attribute.

IT WORKED FOR
THESE THREE CHURCHES

Let's consider the storytelling culture of three different congregations. You will see that each of these churches had an already-established way for implementing an offering time. Some churches are more organic in their approach, and others are more methodical. It's no surprise that each approach seems to reflect the leadership style of the senior pastor. So, all three of these churches approach storytelling in different ways. They are aware of the recommended strategies, but they are also aware of their own congregation's organizational DNA. They've taken the information, created a plan that works for them, and the results have been fruitful.

Several things, however, are *consistent* for these three churches:

- The senior pastoral leadership is fully on board with and actively engaged in creating and implementing the storytelling strategy.

- The leadership's vision for ministry and mission is clear.

- Their weekly worship experiences almost always contain at least one story that connects the offering time with lives changed by God through the financial generosity of God's people.

- Generally, the stories are two minutes or less, with occasional exceptions for longer stories enhanced by video.

One Church Tells Forty "Crazy Compelling" Stories Per Year

This first example is a relatively new church that I've worked with off and on since its birth more than ten years ago. During its early years, the church passed offering baskets in a more traditional way. This practice evolved into basket passing during one of the worship songs while most of the congregation was standing and singing. Then, over time, the church began to take seriously the power of story.

Since then, the worship planning team began meeting on Monday and Wednesday to choose the story for the following Sunday, as well as decide on the placement of the story within the flow of worship—usually just prior to the offering time. For this church, this pre-offering story only happens about eight out of every ten weeks. Why? Because if the team doesn't feel as though they have a story that's going to have an impact, then they shouldn't tell one just to force the issue. The result: about forty stories a year are now told. Here's one that illustrates the "crazy compelling need" that local school children were facing:

> It's come to our attention that the identity of the children in the free and reduced lunch program is obvious to the other children in our county schools. How is it obvious? Because the free and reduced lunch children are all given cold cheese sandwiches while the other children get hot lunches. Let me remind us that our church has a vision of "everyone fed," and our leaders believe that every child in the county school system should have a hot meal for the entire upcoming school year. If you'd like to invest in hot meals for children who are now getting cold cheese sandwiches for lunch, then here's how—

That morning, the pastor invited and challenged the people to give, and they invested *more than enough*—$17,000, in case you're wondering!—so that *every child* in the county currently receiving cheese sandwiches would, instead, receive a hot meal for the entire school year. The next week, the pastor celebrated what God had done through inspiring the people to generosity, and the people gave even more.

"We tell a story of what God is doing here, and the story is so compelling that 'wallets fly open.' People want to invest over and over and over in the thing that we're talking about."

The pastor explains the strategy: "We use the offering moment to invite people to give online in a recurring way. Then we tell a story of what God is doing here, and the story is so compelling that 'wallets fly open.' People want to invest over and over and over in the thing that we're talking about. And they do!"[16]

Now, seven months into the pandemic, this church has reopened for in-person services, with worship attendance still mostly online. No longer are baskets being passed. Instead, they are placed at the entrances/exits and in the lobby area. While they haven't made a final determination, the pastor and executive director anticipate that it will be a very long time, if ever again, that the church will return to passing baskets during worship. They've created a strategy and a rhythm for a better offering.

This Small-Church Pastor Shares a Brief Impact Story Every Week

Leaders of smaller congregations wonder if they have fifty-two stories a year every year to tell. The pastor of one small church decided he only needed to reflect on the many ways that the church impacted the community, so he composed a very short statement to share how the congregation's collective generosity was making a difference. He shared the statement right before the offering time. Some examples of this more abbreviated strategy are:

- "Friends, on three different days this past week, dozens gathered in our building to support one another on a journey of sobriety. Thank you for your generosity, which makes it possible to provide space for those who struggle with alcohol addiction, and for many other recovery and support groups in our town."

- "Did you know that our new playground is helping young families in transition? This week, two parents who just moved their family to town decided to bring their children down the street to enjoy their first time to run and play since a very stressful move. Thank you for generously giving, so we can provide a place for children to laugh and play all week long."

- "I saw a dad and his son this week at the school (six weeks into the school year) and noticed the backpack with a tag on it containing a prayer and our church logo. I commented to the father, 'Nice backpack!' The father replied that a church in town gave it to his son. I introduced myself as the pastor of that church, and the dad exclaimed, 'Thank you so much. My son won't leave the house in the morning until we pray that prayer together. It's the first time we've ever prayed as a family.' Your generosity has not only helped a boy have a brand-new backpack. It has equipped a family to pray every day. Let's keep giving generously, and God will continue to multiply blessings like this in our community."

- "As usual, we had Sunday School last weekend. This Sunday, however, a middle schooler who had never ever been to church before came with one of our students. The class facilitator asked the youth if he had a Bible, and the boy said, 'No, I've never had one before.' The teacher quickly went to the box of Bibles in our curriculum room, got one, and presented it to the student in front of his new friends here at church. I hope that each of you knows that it's through your financial giving that we're able to give Bibles to people of all ages at any time. Thank you for your generosity."

- "This past Thursday was Thanksgiving, and a multi-generational family was playing football on the church's side lawn. I stopped to say hi, and the proud mom of the family greeted me saying, 'We come here every Thanksgiving Day for our Turkey Bowl family tradition. Y'all have the greatest lawn in town, and it's a perfect place for us to work off the turkey feast we've consumed.' Friends, have you noticed how beautiful our lawn and landscaping are? Well, our neighbors have—and your generosity makes it possible for families to enjoy life together on Thanksgiving Day. Because of you, our building and grounds are a blessing to our church and to our community all year long."

These stories provide just a few of the weekly narratives connecting the many ways that the gifts of the people are being used by God to change lives for the better. The pastor is grateful for the opportunity to remind the congregation, one short story at a time, of the ways their collective contributions are being stewarded. He also expresses gratitude for the opportunity to tell these stories in worship, saying, "To tell you the truth, until I started doing this, even I didn't have a full grasp of how the money was being invested and how lives were being impacted for good, one person at a time. It's also made me more excited to connect more deeply with the people of our church and community to hear *more* stories about how God is multiplying our generosity in ways that I could have never imagined. God is good!"

Yes—God is good!

This Church Followed the How-To Guide "By the Book"

The approach of the third congregation illustrates one that closely followed the recommendations of *The How-To Guide for Storytelling in Worship*.

1. They started with a commitment to create a story a week, every week, for at least three months, and then assess the practice.

2. The plan was launched in the summer, typically a low season for attendance and a low season for financial generosity in this particular church.

3. The entire staff was included in the process, and all were equipped with several samples of life-changing stories that clearly connected a changed life with the financial generosity of the people in the church.

4. At the weekly staff meeting, all were invited to submit story content of a paragraph or less—a story that could be read out loud in two minutes or less. Because multiple staff were creating and submitting multiple stories, the church quickly accumulated a list of more than a dozen stories from which to choose.

5. During the weekly staff meeting, one of the agenda items was to map out the stories for the upcoming two to four weekend worship experiences.

6. As suggested in the guide, the preacher for the week was responsible for presenting the content immediately following the conclusion of the message. This also included the responsibility of editing and modifying the content as needed so the narrative would flow out of the message, and also reflect the presentation style of the person telling the story.

7. Per the suggested guide, every story ended with a consistent expression of gratitude: "Thank you for your generosity, which helps stories like this, and so many others, happen through the ministries and mission of our church (followed by instructions for text-to-give, online giving, and placing checks and envelopes in the offering boxes provided any time during the service that day or throughout the week)."

8. The offering time at this church was actually changed to a different place in worship (from before the message to immediately following the message) to ensure that the message would flow right into the life-changing story.

After the three-month trial period, the staff and other leaders never looked back. To this day, the weekly story plants a seed of fruitful ministry into the generous minds and hearts of the church's donors. And storytelling has taken the place of plate-passing! It is exciting to hear that people often come up to the preacher after the service and say, "I really appreciated the story before the offering time today, and I really had no idea that our church was involved in doing something like that."

COULD IT WORK FOR YOUR CHURCH?

Church leaders, *The How-To Guide for Storytelling in Worship* could help *you* create an indigenous process for telling the stories that will inform and inspire your congregation. You can find more information about the guide in the special section at the end of this book. Just one to two minutes a week can be used to communicate information that will increase the understanding of your donors regarding how, through their generosity, God is at work.

It takes the commitment of leaders to try it and the involvement of many to implement it. Through adapting proven steps to create a plan that works for your church and your context, the offering time can become a means of refreshing, weekly inspiration that illustrates the ways that the mission and ministries of your church are impacting lives for the better.

CONVERSATION STARTERS
FOR YOUR TEAM

1. In a highly competitive philanthropic environment, what are the compelling reasons that people give to your church?

2. As we read the life-changing story samples in this chapter, what is one story in your context about a life changed by God through the ministries of your church?

3. Begin to consider: How would the offering time be experienced if you were to incorporate storytelling in lieu of plate-passing?

HABIT 3

REPURPOSE THE OFFERING PLATE AS A VIRTUAL EXPERIENCE

MOROCCO, MUSLIMS, AND A CALL TO PRAYER

In the previous chapter, three different churches were highlighted as examples of how intentional, weekly storytelling in worship led to greater generosity of the people. As understanding increases, and as people are reminded that "God is in the midst of this," then generosity increases. For some donors, this may be a conscious decision to give more as understanding and inspiration increase. For others, however, simply hearing the story may lead to a subconscious desire to invest more.

National Public Radio has a podcast called *Hidden Brain: A Conversation about Life's Unseen Patterns*. In the July 2018 episode, *Creating God*, host Shankar Vedantam tells about a study in which researcher Eric Durham gave money to shopkeepers in Morocco. As he presented the funds, he told the shopkeepers that they could either keep the money or donate the money to charity. He gave some shopkeepers the money during normal business hours, and he gave others the money during the highly audible Muslim call to prayer—a five-times-a-day occurrence.

There is power in any audible cue that
reminds people that God is among them.

In the results of the study, Durham observed that, generally speaking, the shopkeepers were quite charitable and generous. Durham states, "But when the call to prayer was audible, *everybody gave all the money to charity.*" He continued, "It's the most remarkably consistent finding that I've seen. It was a remarkable effect that this audible cue of religion actually had on people."[17]

There is power in any audible cue that reminds people that God is among them, and that they are called to be in relationship with the Creator of the universe. Once again, telling the story—even a short story just before the offering segment of the worship experience—can be an audible source of inspiration that points God's people toward greater generosity.

A DECISION WORTH
DISCERNMENT AND CONVERSATION

Since it's been proven that there is power in story, this book suggests to church leaders that exchanging plate-passing for storytelling can grow the culture of generosity in the church. Giving up such a longstanding practice will likely be met with resistance, but as with any change in any organization where human beings are involved, it may be difficult—not doing something that we've always done can be especially hard.

When March 2020 arrived, however, almost every church in America stopped doing a lot of things that they had always done. Before that time, churches had gathered in person for worship and performed certain functions we were suddenly not able to do:

- Choir members were not able to rehearse and sing together in the same room.

- Childcare at the church facility ceased.

- Hospitality teams were not opening doors and welcoming people into a church building.

- Small groups, children's, and student ministries stopped meeting in-person.

- Attendance pads, registration cards, or "connect" cards were not physically filled out.

- Ushers were not able to pass physical plates to receive checks, cash, envelopes, *I Give Online* cards, or anything else we asked people to put in the containers.

From that time for the months that followed, through the creativity and commitment and persistence of church leaders and members, church happened, just in a different, virtual way.

The pandemic revealed much about the soul of our churches. As a strategist who, in a given year, will interface with dozens of different congregations across the country, I have been amazed at the wondrous ways that the pandemic revealed the "whatever it takes" attitude of church leaders and the congregations with which I have the privilege to be in ministry. Churches that felt stuck discovered they were quite capable of being what they needed to be in order to meet the challenges they never dreamed they would face. Ultimately, the pandemic revealed the nature of who our respective churches really were and are.

In January 2019, Gil Rendle released the book *Quietly Courageous: Leading the Church in a Changing World*. It has been instrumental in my work with helping churches as they consider their vision for the future. More specifically, *Quietly Courageous* is a resource to guide church leaders in discerning the impact they believe their churches are being called to make in their communities and in the world.

In addition, Rendle and his associate, Alice Mann, wrote *Holy Conversations: Strategic Planning as Spiritual Practice for Congregations* where they share a process they created called Holy Conversations, through which church leaders could navigate a season of discernment. At the heart of the Holy Conversations process are three primary questions for church leaders to consider:

1. Who are we as a congregation *now?*

2. Who are our neighbors *now?*

3. What is God calling us to do *now?*

Let's take a closer look at these important questions.

Who are we as a congregation now? The pandemic revealed much about the identity of who our churches are *now*! Some of us have been amazed at what's been revealed, and some have been troubled. I suspect that most of us have been both amazed and troubled in varying measure, but a global virus has invited us to reflect on who we are as a church in ways that we may not have otherwise considered. Rendle suggests that who we are now is not who we once were because the world in which we are doing ministry is not what it once was. And because the world is never going back to what it used to be—what many people call "the good ol' days"—it's a good idea to stop and identify the realities of the now. Our congregation is never going to be like it used to be. It is important for the church to say, "We need to redefine ourselves in order to discern how to move forward in light of the new realities in a different kind of world."

Who are our neighbors now? Because our world is different, the people in the midst of whom our church is planted are different. Perhaps a global crisis has caused us to take a closer look at who our neighbors are. We may have even met some of our neighbors for the first time because everyone has been sheltered-in-place close to home. Hopefully, we have been able to consider not only how we can be a blessing to them, but how they can be a blessing to us. [18]

Who are your neighbors, and how
are you forming lasting relationships
with these children of God?

John Thornburg, a colleague of Rendle's and a facilitator in the Holy Conversations process, wrote a monograph, *Holy Conversation: The "Hard" Is What Makes It Great.* In it, Thornburg challenges church leaders to see mission and ministry to our neighbors as more than just doing things for others, but rather building lasting relationships. Only then will we discover that there is a lot they will give to us if we would be open to receiving it. In the vulnerability of a pandemic/post-pandemic world, can we see that we as a church and our neighbors are connected through God's Spirit as a part of the larger human family? It is through forming lasting relationships with our neighbors that we will discover that not only do our neighbors need us, but we also need our neighbors!

For Thornburg, the "hard" is in having a holy conversation in which an awareness of God's Spirit opens the team to discern, name, and claim things that would not have been uncovered without the difficult work of listening for God's direction. Thornburg shares a story that captures the power of the conversation and the change that can happen in a church that is stuck in its ways of doing ministry.

> In a church which had served a Sunday night meal to home-less neighbors for years, a team member asked a neighbor-hood police captain, "Do you know about our ministry to the homeless?" Little did he expect to hear the police offi-cer to say, "I do, but do you know what happens to those people after they leave the church on Sunday night? And are you actually proud of the fact that you are serving a second generation of the same families on Sunday night?" Though the officer's candor stung at first, being willing to seek the wisdom of the "outsider" steered this church away from its solitary approach to ministry and toward a collec-tive impact strategy with other churches and non-profits.[19]

So, who are your neighbors, and how are you forming lasting rela-tionships with these children of God? Now *that's* a question that could lead to a holy conversation!

What is God calling us to do now? Perhaps the greatest challenge of the Holy Conversations process is doing the work of discernment in order to listen to the Spirit's direction. What are we to do in order to honor who we are now and who our neighbors are now? During the shelter-in-place months of 2020, I had the opportunity to sit virtually with the leaders of two congregations and engage in the Holy Conversations process. As their church buildings were closed, these leaders decided that there was no better time than now to take a long and honest look at their respec-tive responses to the questions of Holy Conversations. By Zoom, we engaged in hours of conversations to seek clarity for a future with hope.

The Spirit has the power to work in the midst of a different kind of season to help us discern what we need to discern in order to move us beyond church business as usual, or as Rendle calls it, our self-appointed preferences.[20] Many of our leaders can't wait to get back to in-person worship in sanctuaries and worship centers so we can do church the way we were doing in February 2020. It is certainly human for us to be tempted with such thinking, but this time is a great opportunity for us to envision a different way to be the church in order to be in ministry in the midst of a different kind of world.

You have an opportunity to create a transformational giving experience rather than the transactional experience to which you may have become accustomed.

What does all of this have to do with passing offering plates? Well, the physical offering plate is symbolic of a weekly exercise that has continued much like it has been for decades, even though the means of giving have drastically changed through the years. It is a representation of our tendency to do things, as a church, according to our self-appointed preferences instead of considering that how we are doing things may not fit the culture of the people we serve and the people we are called to reach.

In the offering segment of the weekly worship service, you have an opportunity to create a transformational giving experience rather than the transactional experience to which you may have become accustomed. And there's no time like now to be in conversation about what that would mean in your particular context.

AN OPPORTUNITY TO
LIVE INTO THE VISION NOW!

Over the past twenty years, I've had the privilege of coaching more than seventy-five new church start pastors and their leaders. During the pandemic, I had a conversation with one of those leaders: the founding pastor of a twelve-year-old congregation. In response to the question, "What are you learning right now?" the pastor responded, "We're learning that things we had envisioned doing two years from now are things that we can begin to live into right now, not in spite of COVID-19 but because of COVID-19."[21] This is a church with a vision for multiplication. Its leaders had been planning to launch a virtual campus in a couple of years, but as everyone mobilized and sheltered in place, the vision for the future—by the power and inspiration of God's Spirit—was being fulfilled in the now!

The moral to the story is: Once you give up a practice that you believe to be essential, you may just discover that the loss opens the door to a greater purpose you may never have realized if not for the loss. You may discover that what you deemed essential wasn't essential at all. It was just a preference with which you and others had become comfortable.

This new vision for a better offering is one where the passing of the plate during in-person worship goes away. Had I suggested this possibility in February 2020, I'm guessing there would have been very limited interest—to some, it would have been too radical. And I confess, I may not have written this particular book had it not been for this year of change. As a company, our strategists were already working with the thousands of congregations to grow electronic giving. But growing e-giving would have been suggested as a practice *in addition to* and not in place of passing the plate.

Enter the coronavirus, and for month after month after month, churches were able to be the church without meeting in person. Many churches struggled financially, but the churches with already-established practices of storytelling (stories that clearly connected financial contributions to life-changing ministry) were actually able to thrive.

One thing consistent for almost every congregation in America: however long your season of virtual worship lasted, you were able to be the church and fund the ministry of the church in some measure without physically passing the plate during worship.

Is it time to transition toward a strategy in the life of the church where the offering plate doesn't need to be passed anymore? Even more emphatically, could it actually increase the generosity of your church by replacing it with storytelling that inspires and motivates your people to invest more in the work of God?

A CHALLENGE TO CHURCH LEADERS FOR A BETTER OFFERING

Vanco Payment Solutions helps to escort churches into the twenty-first century by providing e-giving services. In a pre-pandemic survey by Vanco, 82 percent of respondents stated that the practice of passing the offering plate was a part of the worship service they typically attended. In an article by Kevin Lee, Vanco's CEO, he reminds us of some other trends in America:

- From 2000 to 2015—a five-year period—pay-by-check declined by 50 percent to 19.4 billion checks per year.

- During the same period, payments made through credit cards, direct deposit, and other services tripled to 103.3 billion transactions per year.

- Most Americans carry less than $50 with them and 40 percent have less than $20 with them at any given time.[22]

So, pay-by-check has been rapidly declining in America, credit card and electronic payments are rapidly increasing, and churches should be ready right now to receive gifts online and through other electronic means.

At this point, it's important for me to say that your church may be struggling in the area of growing electronic giving through its website, text-to-give, and other e-giving platforms. If this is the case, the resources are abundant to guide you into the present-day philanthropic marketplace. Tools are available to help you grow electronic giving even as you celebrate gifts that are given through more traditional means. Richard Rogers has been my go-to person regarding this important means of establishing a healthy culture of giving in church. His book, *The E-Giving Guide for Every Church: Using Digital Tools to Grow Ministry*, has been a blessing to me, my church ministry partners, and countless churches across the country.

> Tools are available to help you grow electronic giving even as you celebrate gifts that are given through more traditional means.

So—should *your* church stop passing the plate during worship? While I'm challenging church leaders to discern what their particular answer to this question should be (after all, you know you better than I know you), here are some additional reasons that build my case for ceasing a practice that is likely no longer productive and actually may be counter-productive to growing the financial generosity of your church.

1. **E-giving honors the scriptural invitation to "bring the offering"** versus "have someone collect the offering from you" (see Psalm 96:8 and Malachi 3:10). Perhaps others feel differently, but "collection plates" implies that our giving is taken or received by the collector (the usher) who approaches the giver in order to collect it on behalf of the organization (the church). "Bringing" the offering, however, implies that the movement is incumbent on the donor. As

the offering is brought, it is out of the giver's need to give rather than the need for the church to receive.

2. **We have survived—even thrived—during a season without plate-passing.** During a season of virtual worship, we didn't pass a physical plate, and worship was meaningful and creatively planned and celebrated among the scattered people who gathered online. At the very least, this season has invited us to assess many long-cherished practices that may no longer fit the mission related to growing disciples and reaching new people, in addition to more people and new kinds of people. One of those practices is passing the plate.

3. **Checks and cash are no longer the preferred means of making payments for most transactions, including shopping, bill paying, dining, etc.** Plate-passing was designed with checks and cash in mind, but this practice no longer accommodates the typical donor in today's world. New protocols for giving should be influenced by the language of giving for the modern world and the modern church.

Giving as an act of worship can happen any time and any place.

---

4. **There are other more creative and inspiring ways to ensure that the offering time is a true act of worship, not a routine ritual.** While waiting for the passing of a physical plate, our minds can wander and lose focus on the motivations for giving. Hearing inspiring, true stories about the impact of generosity draws and holds our minds to the very reason and purpose we not only are to give but want to give.

5. **Repurposing the offering into a time of storytelling creates an invitation for people to give in a variety of ways, according to their respective preferences.** How can the current offering time be repurposed into an inspirational, informational, transformational time of gratitude and response? Because there are many ways to give—text-to-give, online through the church website or app, automatic funds transfer (AFT), giving cash or a check during or after the service, and mailing a check or bringing it by the church during the week. Giving as an act of worship can happen any time and any place. This means that an offering container is something that should always be available and ready to receive the gifts that are brought by whatever means and at whatever time inspired by God in the donor. All of these methods can be means of giving as an act of worship. As I've said, during the closing of church buildings in 2020, worship did not stop, and mission and ministry did not come to a halt. "Act of worship" has not needed to happen in a particular place or space. And if this is true during a pandemic, then it has always been true and always will be true no matter our circumstances.

A GIFT FROM AFRICA
AND MY AUNT BETTY JEAN

Years ago, a friend of mine traveled to Ghana, Africa. As with most mission-related trips, he went to teach and preach and ended up learning more than he could have ever taught. He was more inspired than inspiring (though he is an awesome preacher!). One of the highlights of the trip for him was the offering time at one of the worship services where he was preaching. He was expecting an offering time much like the one his church back home—slow moving, awkward pauses, mostly meditative music, and lacking energy. Instead, he was blown away by the experience in the open-air Ghanaian service. When it was time for the offering, the people began to sing, dance, and clap their hands to the celebrative music. Moved by the Spirit, God's people spontaneously made their way toward the front of the space where two handmade pottery containers were located. Most worshipers placed portions of their offerings in both containers. Some came forward and danced past the containers without placing anything inside. Some acted as if they were placing something in the containers, but their hands were empty as they waved them over the container openings. Following the service, the pastor explained that one of the containers was designated for offerings to God for the church, and the other container was designated for offerings to God for the poor in their community. Following worship, the offering container for the poor was taken into the village, and there, the contributions were distributed to anyone who had need.

As my friend recounted this story from years past, his face lit up and his voice reflected the passion and inspiration of the experience. Now, as I reflect on his story, I lament at what the offering time has become in so many of the churches I attend every year. Perhaps a story from Ghana could inspire us as it has inspired others for

- bringing our gifts to God is an act of worship;

- bringing our gifts to God is an occasion to celebrate, sing, and dance;

- bringing our gifts to God is a time of offering our *whole* selves—including our financial gifts—to our Creator, whether our resources are abundant or empty;

- bringing our gifts to God is an opportunity to support the church and remember those in need; and

- bringing our gifts to God is a reason to praise, regardless of our circumstances.

The writer of Hebrews 13:15 casts a vision for a never-ending, joy-filled offering, and not just an offering of money, but an offering of our whole selves to God: "Through [Jesus], then, let us continually offer a sacrifice of praise to God... the fruit of lips that profess his name" (NRSV).

> *We are the sacrifice of praise* in the ways that we live and the ways that we offer every part of ourselves for the work of the Creator in the world.

This brings to mind my Aunt Betty Jean—she was a saint. She endured much in her life, and as a relatively young woman, she was diagnosed with terminal cancer. Even in her last days, she insisted on attending worship at church. A few days before she died, she was too weak to walk but not too weak to request that she be taken to the church for the weekly worship experience. My uncle carried her frail body into the worship center, and the service began with the Maranatha chorus inspired by Hebrews 13:15, "We Bring the Sacrifice of Praise."[23] When the service was over, as she was being carried back to the car, she struggled to speak the words that, to this day, offer inspiration and hope for my journey. Aunt Betty Jean, a beloved child of God ready for the transition from life to life-beyond-life, whispered, "I am the sacrifice of praise."

Praise is our offering as we bring our whole selves into God's house. And God's house, ultimately, is *anywhere* that God is. We are to bring the sacrifice of praise. *We are the sacrifice of praise* in the ways that we live and the ways that we offer every part of ourselves for the work of the Creator in the world.

It is interesting to me that when in the presence of the vulnerable, in the presence of the impoverished, in the presence of the dying, we are able to see more clearly the freedom that this kind of offering—the offering of our whole lives—can bring.

May the sacrificial offerings that we bring be done in a spirit of generosity, praise, celebration, and gratitude.

PUTTING IT ALL TOGETHER—A NEW WAY OF OFFERING ALL WEEK LONG

We've discussed the importance of discernment and the power of life-changing stories through generous giving. We've confirmed that people have a variety of means through which to make a contribution and the importance of the church's ability to receive all forms of giving. Furthermore, donors should be invited to give in ways that enable their particular contribution to be offered out of a sense of gratitude and as an act of worship.

So, what will *a better offering* look like? Of course, the answer to this will vary from church to church. Each congregation has different styles, traditions, and other variables to consider when planning the weekly worship experience. But here are some major points to consider when creating the flow and rhythm of the offering time that works for your church. And in considering all of the churches across the country—where I'm able to be a part of worship throughout the year—here are some suggested components ordered in a way that can help in your discernment process.

1. **Lead with a story about a life changed by God through the financial generosity of God's people.** Highlight how life transformation has occurred as a result of God's power working through a ministry of your church. Tell the story in two minutes or less through a written narrative (which could be supported by photos) or by video. Because we're talking about fifty-two stories per year, be aware of your

church's capabilities or potential limitations for video and editing, and "think simple" from the beginning. There is power in a well-crafted one- to two-minute written narrative that focuses on one person or one family's story. Tell it!

2. **Make sure the connection is clear between the life-changing story and the financial generosity of the people.** Significant life transformation happens all around us by the power of God working through God's people. For this purpose, however, it should be obvious and clear to those listening that the work of God in the story is a result of the impact of the Spirit through collective financial generosity of the people.

3. **After the story, say thank you to the people whose collective generosity played a part.** If the grateful hearts of your people led them to financially support the ministry being highlighted, then the natural response of the church should be to express gratitude for those gifts that were then invested well with a fruitful result.

4. **After saying thank you, briefly share how the peoples' continued generosity will multiply the life-changing impact of the church's ministry even more.** In other words, keep the momentum going. Provide instructions for ways to give whether through an offering plate/box/container provided in the worship space, or through other specified electronic means.

5. **Sing a song of gratitude (a brief chorus of praise) as people respond to the invitation to physically or virtually offer their gifts.** This time of offering can involve actual movement during the song (people bringing checks to offering boxes, texting-to-give, or giving through the app, etc.). This

song of gratitude can be a time of celebration or reflection while people are directed to give at any time during worship and that online and other electronic gifts can be contributed as an act of worship 24/7/365.

Affirmed that their gifts have been invested in transformational ways, your people will be compelled to invest more so that the work of God can continue to multiply.

As indicated above, your pattern, rhythm, and timing will vary based on the uniqueness of your particular worship experience. More liturgical traditions often have the offering as a response to the message delivered. This creates an ideal opportunity immediately following the sermon, and the life-changing story can even be facilitated or presented by the person who has just completed the message.

In whatever way it happens, create a flow that, at least in the first two or three months, is consistent. Through the life change shared, many will not only be inspired by the story that is told, but also informed about ministries of the church of which they may not have been aware. Affirmed that their gifts have been invested in transformational ways, your people will be compelled to invest more so that the work of God can continue to multiply through their collective generosity.

ONE CHURCH'S DISCERNMENT FOR A BETTER OFFERING

In preparing for the gradual re-opening—seven months into the pandemic—one congregation engaged in a deliberate process of discernment regarding many of the church's pre-pandemic practices. One of these practices was the passing of the plate. The conversation began with the simple question, "How long will it be before we'll be able to have the ushers pass the plates for the offering time?" At first, the knee-jerk response to this question became, "Whenever there is a vaccination for COVID-19." A doctor reminded the discernment team that many studies indicate that the current flu shot is effective only 70 percent of the time, plus there's no guarantee that everyone will get the shot. Then the team began to wonder if their church would ever pass plates among hundreds of people again.

The list of questions expanded:

- How many people are actually putting something into the plate when it's handed to them?

- If we don't pass the plate, are the ever-shrinking percentage of people who *do* put something in going to be confused or offended?

- What about our first-time guests? What will they think when the mostly empty plate reaches them, especially the ones at the back of the worship center?

- What should we do?

The surface conversation was an important beginning to the discernment process. And then it happened: not long into the conversation, the church leaders began to ask much deeper questions, beginning with, "What is the purpose of the offering time anyway?" After further conversation, the agreed-upon answer was multi-faceted. The purpose of the offering time is

1. to provide a designated time to acknowledge that God has richly blessed us, and to give a portion of our financial blessings back to the One who ultimately is the Owner of all our resources;

2. to create space during which people are invited to consider the work of God and want to partner with God in multiplying the fruit of our common ministry and mission; and

3. to help those present to discover the joy of generosity in every area of their lives.

These answers then led to a few more questions:

- Does our typical offering time help us to fulfill these purposes?

- Is how we've been doing it for a very long time still helping us to fulfill our purpose of honoring God and helping others grow in the grace of giving?

Well, as you know, change is hard, and the conversation for this particular church was not an easy one. But for them, the ever-decreasing use of the physical offering plate ultimately inspired them to conclude a number of things.

- They could at least acknowledge that it would be a very long time before they passed anything down the rows, *especially* the offering plates.

- If they weren't going to pass physical offering plates—possibly never again—how would they create an offering experience that is safe and fulfills the purposes they had outlined?

> Even through a pandemic, God doesn't waste a single wilderness experience.

Church leaders, if you can at least acknowledge that it's going to be a very long time before you pass anything among the people, then perhaps it's time to have a deeper conversation about the purposes of why you do what you do. In a virtual world with electronic payments becoming the norm, you have the opportunity to create a refreshing approach that's relevant to the current world in which you and your people live. You still have ongoing opportunity to honor God and God's life-changing work in your midst and through the generosity of your people—that will never change.

I have been reminded that even through a pandemic, God doesn't waste a single wilderness experience. In the song *Beautiful Things*, Lisa and Michael Gungor remind us that God not only can make beautiful things out of dust, God will make beautiful things out of us.[24] Through this world's season of sickness and death and uncertainty, the old is passing away (see Revelation 21:1–5), and God is recreating us into something new. And as old things pass away in the wilderness of this pandemic and its post-season, God is working through us a new way that can lead to a garden of generosity.

CONVERSATION STARTERS FOR YOUR TEAM

1. How would your congregation feel about engaging in a season of "holy conversations" to honestly address the questions: Who are we (as a church) *now*; who are our neighbors *now*; and what is God calling us to do *now*?

2. Are you willing to list the ministries and practices of your church and evaluate whether they are mostly driven by a self-appointed preference or a compelling desire to follow the leading of God's Spirit?

3. What questions should you be asking as a means of reshaping the offering time so the experience leads to increased generosity in your church?

CREATE AN ALL-YEAR GENEROSITY PLAN FOR YOUR CHURCH

IMPLEMENT THAT ONE THING, THEN MOVE ON TO THE NEXT

This fourth habit is content-rich and helps to create an all-year generosity strategy for your church. When taken as a whole, it may seem overwhelming, but as with creating any comprehensive strategy, success begins by doing one thing well and then building on it by adding another component and then another until the full strategy is in place.

In my early days of ministry, I recall going to multi-day conferences and being flooded with ideas, advice, and information overload. Drinking from the proverbial fire hose, I would typically find myself overwhelmed and discouraged halfway into the first day! I forget where the encouragement came from, but I recall hearing someone say, "For me, I come to an event like this with the hope of finding one thing that inspires me to either make a change in me or a change in the church

I'm serving. Then, once that idea or inspiration has had its effect on my ministry, I may be able to implement something else beneficial. But if I can just bring home one useful concept or strategy, then the trip has been well worth it!"

For this chapter, I invite you to find the one thing that resonates— the one thing that is applicable for you based on how you naturally lead. It should be the one thing that can be adapted to your ministry environment in a fruitful, impactful way. My sense is that if you're able to find that one thing, then the inspiration and motivation will naturally be there for moving on to the next thing—and the next.

REMEMBER: THERE ARE FOUR POCKETS OF GIVING

When Clif Christopher wrote *Not Your Parents' Offering Plate* more than ten years ago, he focused on the three pockets of giving: annual giving, capital giving, and planned giving. Today, church leaders continue to witness the propensity of donors to invest in specific projects, ministries, and missions that align with their passions for the work of God through their local church. Because of this shift, I'm adding a fourth pocket of giving called special giving—a.k.a. "designated giving." Though special giving is nothing new to churches, it has often been removed from the generosity conversation out of concern that, if people in the church were invited to invest *only* in those things that appealed to them, they may give 100 percent of their contributions as special, designated gifts.

What I have discovered over the past fifteen years of serving as a generosity strategist is that if giving is communicated well within the church throughout the year, all four pockets of giving have a place within the ongoing generosity conversation. Ultimately, we want the households in our church to be well-informed about all available options for giving. Donors should then be invited and equipped with the information needed to give in the way they feel inspired and led by the Spirit, in whatever ways they feel compelled.

Let's take a look at the four pockets of giving in a way that communicates the importance of each and how all four can come together to create a holistic culture of generosity in the church.

Pocket 1: Annual Giving

On the surface, annual giving supports the ongoing, foundational work of the church. It is foundational because it funds the day-to-day life of the church in order for the church to function well. Annual giving supports the fixed costs such as:

- Building and grounds (cleaning, maintenance, repair, insurance, etc.)

- Utilities

- Staff (salaries, benefits, expenses)

- Basic ministries and missions

> No longer are people giving generously just because they're supposed to, and no longer is there an assumed trust and confidence that donor dollars will be stewarded well.

In making the case for annual giving, it is important not only to communicate what the money supports, but how the general contributions of the people are invested in life-changing ways. Remember, we have transitioned away from being the church where people gave annual gifts because they were *supposed* to give them. Once upon a time, most donors gave weekly, monthly, quarterly, or annually, not because they knew where the money was going, but because they generally believed that the church couldn't operate without these gifts. And likely, there was a certain level of trust that these gifts would be stewarded responsibly in order for the church operate. Back in the day, donors gave because they believed they were supposed to give, they believed that the church needed their gifts, they took seriously the biblical references to giving, and they had a very high level of trust and confidence that their gifts would be responsibly stewarded.

So much about this dynamic has changed!

In our divergent culture, people are actually being drawn away from larger groups and communities such as the church. There is also a higher level of suspicion of donors toward any organization because of past stories of mismanagement and misuse of funds. There is a more individualistic mindset on giving instead of a communal sense of obligation. This means that with giving to any organization—including the church—there is either a stated or a subconscious need to know more about how the money is being spent. And because of the nonspecific nature of how gifts placed in the literal or metaphorical offering plate will be handled, there is a diminishing motivation for a donor to place funds into such a container. By and large, no longer are people giving generously just because they're supposed to, and no longer is there an assumed trust and confidence that donor dollars will be stewarded well. In the twenty-first century, such trust and confidence *must be built* through intentional means of communication.

The primary focus of weekly storytelling should connect the ways that *annual giving* provides the foundational funding for the church.

One thing that has remained consistent both then and now is that the church has an opportunity like *no other non-profit* organization.

The people of the church gather weekly (online or in-person) for worship, and anywhere from 25 to 50 percent of the supporters of the church will show up in worship on any given weekend or throughout the week. So when the time comes to invite people to invest in the ongoing work of God in the church, how will its leaders connect the offering time with the lives that have been changed through the annual gifts being sought? If trust needs to be established, then how will this confidence be built?

I have gone to great lengths to point church leaders toward weekly storytelling with the understanding that most of the stories will connect the minds and hearts of generous *annual giving* donors to lives changed by God for the better. Other stories told will celebrate how donated *capital giving* has resulted in changed lives. Still others will highlight *special giving* and its positive impact on peoples' lives. *Planned giving*, especially when it becomes a part of a church's generosity culture, can be celebrated as gifts that are already having life-changing impact and will continue to make a difference for generations to come. But the primary focus of weekly storytelling should connect the ways that *annual giving* provides the foundational funding for the church.

In a healthy environment of generosity, each pocket of giving has its proper place. This will be evident in the narrative of the church as it invites people to give in the ways they feel led by God to give. And it will be evident in the minds and hearts of the donors as they faithfully respond to the invitation to live a holistically generous life.

Think about annual giving this way:

- **It's not just about the upkeep of the building and grounds.** Instead, what if we were able to identify the countless lives changed, one person at a time, because, during any given week, seven days a week, fifty-two weeks a year, every year, people walk onto the campus and into the facilities to learn about Jesus; to make a decision to follow Jesus; to be inspired by the Spirit; to hear a message of unconditional love; to recover from addiction; to find a new friend; to connect with long-time friends; to experience healing from brokenness; to learn more about the Bible; to find a better way to live? Having a home base of ministry and mission provides a place for all of this to happen, and through the generosity of God's people, most churches are able to provide such a place.

Could we consider eliminating the words *programs* and *programming* from the church's vocabulary?

- **It's not just about the utility bills.** I mean, how inspiring is that? Not very! Instead, what if donors were invited to connect with lives that have changed because people have a safe, comfortable place in which to let their guard down and explore a deeper faith, connect with others who may have similar struggles, and even make a difference in someone else's life? One pastor, prior to the offering, told the story of a woman who had never donated blood, but when she saw the sign outside the church asking for much-needed blood because of the pandemic, she felt led to give. She entered the facility and found the chapel, which had been converted into a very large "blood mobile" where people could give in a socially distanced, climate-controlled environment. She not only gave blood, she gave plasma. And the pastor concluded the offering appeal by saying, "Friends, thank you for your generosity, which enabled us to open our facility so the blood center could provide a comfortable, air-conditioned place for making donations and saving peoples' lives." It's not just about utilities, is it? It's about lives being saved.[25]

- **It's not just about staff salaries.** It's about the ways that God works through the people who answer a call to ministry, whether it be a pastor, administrative assistant, director of missions, or the custodial staff. It isn't a stretch at all to know that each and every day, God works through the staff—all week, not just on Sundays—and that the peoples' generosity funds each of the staff's salaries.

- **It's not just about programs.** By the way, could we consider eliminating the words *programs* and *programming* from the church's vocabulary? Other non-profit organizations may provide programs for children, youth, or adults, but the church is empowered by God to life-changing *mission* and *ministry!* Telling a story each week places a human face on the transformational work of the Spirit and emphasizes the effectiveness of each mission or ministry. In turn, people better understand how their contributions are being invested.

Weekly stories help heighten the understanding and confidence of the people and their giving. An if people are inspired to support the general ministries and missions of the church, then making the case for the other three pockets of giving is much easier and *a lot* less threatening.

Historically, church leaders have struggled to connect the weekly offering appeal to life-changing ministry, so the special giving pocket has almost been ignored for fear that it would compete with annual giving. And since annual giving is foundational to the basic, ongoing work of God through the church, the other three pockets of giving do not get the microphone time that the annual pocket receives.

Church leaders continue to fear that contributions given to the other three pockets of giving will diminish the annual pocket. However, attention to *all four* pockets will ultimately help a church realize its generosity capacity. So let's look briefly at the other three pockets of giving.

Pocket 2: Capital Giving

Capital giving provides funds for securing or upgrading the assets related to the church's property and facilities. Capital campaigns, therefore, are typically for the purpose of buying land, building new buildings, expanding existing buildings, renovating facilities, or reducing/ eliminating long-term debt. Practically, if annual contributions are invested in the day-to-day ministries and mission of the church, capital contributions are used to acquire or restore an asset of the church. In doing so, a capital gift will have a long-term, generational, or even a lifetime impact on the church's ministry.

If you've ever been in a sanctuary during the heat of the summer when one of the air conditioning systems (a capital asset) fails, then you realize that, in a very tangible way, the capital gifts given to replace that asset will have a life-changing impact! The same goes for the beauty of a stained-glass window, which brings comfort or inspiration. Or what about the newly remodeled check-in area for children's ministry, which inspires confidence that the children will be cared for in a safe, secure environment. Capital assets are a part of the life-changing work of God through the church, and these improvements are made possible through God's Spirit working through the generosity of God's people.

When seasoned church leaders hear the word *capital*, they typically associate it with a multi-month campaign where households are invited to make multi-year commitments that are over and above annual giving in order to fulfill the vision of the church. Some leaders get excited about opportunities such as this. Some, however, have experienced donor fatigue, especially if they've been part of a church that overbuilt, went into too much debt, or ended up in back-to-back-to-back capital campaigns. In the words of one campaign-weary church leader, "We thought, *build it and they will come,* but we built it and they didn't come." These church leaders ended up having five, back-to-back, capital campaigns. They did not have a positive feeling about the word *capital.*

Positive feelings or not, capital expenditures are important for churches that have land and buildings. And there *are* people in the church who are passionate about updating and/or upgrading the facilities and systems that maximize the life-changing impact of assets. For people who are especially committed to caring for the building and grounds, the capital funding opportunities need to be communicated—just as the annual funding plan is communicated—so potential donors will understand the impact of both.

Now, just because capital gifts are important doesn't mean a church needs a campaign. This chapter will provide some ways that capital giving can be included *in the flow* of the ongoing fundraising narrative of the church.

A friend of mine pastors a church in the Southeast. When he first arrived, there was more than $1 million in deferred maintenance that needed to be done. For more than a decade, the ministries and mission of the church had been faithfully funded while the building and grounds of the church fell into disrepair. Under their new pastor's visionary guidance, the leaders finally saw the need for a capital campaign, but they still viewed the building and grounds as being separate from the mission and ministry of the church.

> Your building and grounds have missionary status—they are a part of the front-line first impressions team.

One day, a man experiencing homelessness who was a part of the congregation was enjoying a beautiful morning in the church courtyard—something he did frequently. He was sitting on a bench surrounded by rotting courtyard columns when the pastor walked by and struck up a conversation, as he had done many times before. As they spoke, the man gazed upward with fascination at the church's historic bell tower, which needed significant repair. He pointed excitedly toward the tower and blurted out, "That bell is a missionary!"

The pastor said, "A missionary? Say more."

"Pastor, every day, the bell calls out to the community and reminds people of God's love. I tell you, that bell is a missionary!"

Do you grasp the words of this insightful child of God? Your building and grounds have missionary status—they are a part of the frontline first impressions team. They communicate the welcome, the beauty, and the unconditional acceptance of the Creator, or at least they should. Truly, God uses your church building and its grounds every single week to bring the message of love and grace to a world in need. And it's through capital giving that the vital function of your building and grounds is maximized.

Churches continue to stand on the philanthropic sideline while other institutional non-profits cultivate and receive substantial planned gifts from their supporters.

Pocket 3: Planned Giving

Planned giving provides an opportunity for donors to give a lasting legacy gift that has a life-changing impact far beyond the donor's life on earth. Think about it—who would want to invest in the church they love beyond their lifetime? I suspect that the answer is "I do!" for a majority of Jesus followers. Even so, a small minority of people are ever actually invited to do so. Therefore, a very small percentage of people who have been active in the life of the church give a planned gift to support the work of God after their death.

As noted earlier, most charitable organizations are envious that churches are able to make a weekly financial appeal to their gathered supporters. However, churches continue to stand on the philanthropic sideline while colleges, universities, and other institutional non-profits cultivate and receive substantial planned gifts from their supporters. The biggest difference between planned giving in churches and other charitable organizations is simple: many organizations ask their donors to remember them in their will—and then provide the expertise and resources to help this happen. Other organizations, including most churches, never get around to even inviting their donors to make a planned gift.

Interestingly enough, because most planned gifts align with the donor's passion for ministry, the legacy gift can be specified as an annual, capital, and/or special gift! Establishing and growing a legacy (endowment) ministry of the church is easy. In creating an all-year narrative for legacy gifts, churches can create a strategy for inviting their donors to consider planned gifts, which is the most overlooked pocket of giving.

"I support the annual fund of the church because I love my church. I give extra to the student ministries of the church because the youth ministry where I grew up saved my life."

Pocket 4: Special Giving

Special giving provides opportunities for people to invest in areas for which each donor has a passion. In a healthy ministry environment, these gifts are given above and beyond the annual support of the church. Special gifts allow households to invest financially in places where they have more of an investment personally or spiritually. I heard a generous layperson once state, "I support the annual fund of the church because I love my church. I give extra to the student ministries of the church because the youth ministry where I grew up saved my life. I want to invest with the knowledge and the hope that lives are being saved through our student ministries." We've talked about a life changed— how about a life *saved*? This donor was highly motivated to give a special gift because of his personal experience with that ministry.

While special giving opportunities align a donor's passion with the church's vision, there are challenges that come with this pocket of giving. Special giving is sometimes used when a donor becomes disgruntled with the pastor or church leaders. Or it may happen when the donor's confidence or trust erodes concerning previous stewardship of the general contributions (annual giving). As a result of this concern, annual giving could reduce or completely stop, and in its place, the donor could specify only special (designated) funds with their contributions. As a former pastor, you might guess my feelings about what appears to be a tactic of conditional generosity. I've actually heard people say, "If I like what you're doing, then I'm going to give. If not, then I won't."

Through the years, however, I have come to a place where I look at this dynamic differently. Ultimately, I believe that the conviction of financial giving is between the giver and God. Through a journey of prayerful discernment, people should seek and discover God's direction and take God's lead. Giving, after all, is a response of gratitude, prayer, and faith.

The following spiritual principle of giving was introduced by Kristine Miller and Scott McKenzie in their book *Bounty: Ten Ways to Increase Giving at Your Church*. McKenzie and Miller affirm that, as people genuinely embark on a journey of gratitude, prayer, and faith, they will discern what generosity looks like for them, and they will do what they believe the Spirit is leading them to do.[26]

Three words: *gratitude, prayer, and faith*: Have you considered that all generosity is *grounded in gratitude*? In my own journey of generosity, it is from a sense of heartfelt gratitude that my discernment process for giving begins. In seeking God's direction, I prayerfully consider what my response should be in each situation. This is because God's direction is *revealed in prayer*. Prayer is the primary means by which I discover God's will—in this case, for a decision about giving. Then, as I discern God's will, generosity will flow from God through me, because giving is a faith decision. So generosity is *lived in faith*.

Churches that inspire generosity are able to create an environment of discernment where donors are invited on their own journey of gratitude, prayer, and faith. In response, people will financially support the church in the way they believe their Creator is directing them. As church leaders, you have the opportunity to provide this environment of prayerful discernment for the people in your church and for yourselves.

Another challenge with special giving is that, as a church changes, many things that were part of the church's life decades ago are no longer a primary focus or even a focus at all. One example of this is a church that had a pipe organ in its sanctuary, and over time, the organ fell into disrepair. To restore the organ would have cost more than a million dollars. Meanwhile, the organ fund accumulated to more than $150,000. As the congregation continued to decline in attendance, membership, and giving, several of their special funds had become both substantial and untouchable. Without a provision, a policy, or a process for repurposing special funds away from their originally designated ministry/mission, the organ fund continued to grow while other more current needs were not being met. Ironically, the church had the money to invest in new ministry opportunities but decided instead to leave those funds in their designated place. To this day, the church is still in decline, the organ is still not useable, and the organ fund is not only untouchable, it continues to receive designated contributions.

In a healthy congregation, special gifts—even with the potential pitfalls—invite and empower people to give in specific ways they believe the Spirit is calling them to make a greater impact. And because institutional non-profits have created a culture where donors are encouraged to choose exactly where their contribution should be directed, many churches are adopting this strategy as well.

CREATING A RHYTHM FOR ALL-YEAR GENEROSITY WITH ALL FOUR POCKETS

My life has been blessed, and my ministry has been significantly influenced over the years through knowing Clif Christopher, the founder of Horizons Stewardship, which I mentioned earlier. Joe Park, the CEO of Horizons, has truly been a gift and an inspiration to me since I first joined the organization as a strategist in 2006.

Several years ago, Joe unveiled a year-round generosity emphasis that aligned the seasons of the year with the various pockets of giving. This generosity strategy has equipped church leaders to create a rhythm for emphasizing annual giving, along with the other three pockets of giving, all year long! This may seem obvious, but most churches implement an annual giving emphasis for three to four weeks in the fall and then say very little about annual giving the other eleven months of the year. Furthermore, churches may *never* intentionally address capital, planned, and special giving during a typical year.

In addition to having a twelve-month focus on the annual pocket of giving, Joe also helped me understand that there are particular times when the rhythm and seasons of the year create opportunities to focus on the other three pockets of giving. To be clear, any kind of gift can be given at any time during the year. Certain times of the year, however, provide a more natural season for cultivating capital, special, and planned giving. Here are some general notes about the rhythm and narrative for an all-year, four-pocket, generosity plan.

Cultivating Annual Giving

It's not just for the fall! Unless you decided to read this chapter first (I've been known to do that before), you won't be surprised when I say that every single week, you have an opportunity to connect your offering time with a simple story that illustrates how the collective generosity of the people has resulted in a life changed for the better.

Through implementing this storytelling strategy during weekly worship, you are providing dozens of examples per year, every year, of how the people's financial investments in the annual ministry fund are resulting in life transformation. You are putting a human face on the physical, virtual, or metaphorical offering plate. You are growing the understanding of the donor at least once a week. In doing so, you are inspiring the donor to invest more, so any future financial investment will multiply the work of God that is being done in and through the generosity of God's people.

Cultivating Capital Giving

If annual giving should be cultivated throughout the year, one week at a time, capital giving should be cultivated whenever there are capital needs. Periodically, there may be a need for a more intentional capital campaign inviting households to make multi-year commitments for projects (construction, renovation, deferred maintenance), debt retirement, or land purchase.

The reality is that virtually every organization has ongoing capital needs. Therefore, the opportunity for supporters to invest in capital improvements should be ongoing instead of periodic. For many congregations, the tendency is to focus solely on annual fundraising until the capital needs accumulate over time. The result can be a list of deferred capital projects that total anywhere from thousands to millions of dollars.

What if capital needs became an ongoing part of your church's all-year funding narrative? Per Joe Park's guidance, if we think about this against the backdrop of the seasons of the year, then there are at least three times during the year when a capital wish list could be communicated to the households of your church:

1. **Pre-summer:** Prior to June, create a capital wish list that includes projects that could more easily be done during the summer months. Include especially those projects that are best done when attendance is down. Additionally, the wish list might also include projects that would position the church to be ready for the back-to-school season in the fall. Here are some things to consider:

   - parking lot repair (including security lighting)

   - pre-school/children's area improvements

   - sanctuary/worship center projects

   - office renovations

   - signage upgrades

2. **Fall:** Update and distribute the capital wish list during the fall. This list may contain projects that were on the pre-summer list, or newly discovered capital needs, such as a broken water pipe that flooded the children's building or a failing HVAC system. Some items to consider:

   - HVAC upgrades

   - Fall landscaping upgrades

3. **Year-end:** The timing of the release of the updated December capital wish list is strategic and not just because additional items may have been discovered during the fall. As year-end

approaches, there will be households in your church that may have the means and the need to make a large gift prior to the end of the calendar year. Therefore, even if the list for December looks identical to September's, you'll want to distribute the list again.

The people who love Jesus and love your church want to invest in the work of God, but they need to know what the needs are and be invited to invest in them.

This is where I often hear church leaders say, "We don't really want to distribute the capital wish list in December because we don't want capital giving to compete with annual giving during the month when we need to finish the year strong." While I get that—because I've been there myself—I've come to the conclusion that people will give according to where their hearts for ministry are. For some, they are especially committed to funding the ongoing ministry and mission of the church. For others, they are passionate about the buildings and grounds of "God's house" being cared for. Also, those whose financial gifts are coming from accumulated assets often want to invest in something that will have a more lasting impact and are therefore inclined to direct those gifts toward capital projects.

This takes me back to the discernment piece for generosity. If we are intentional to invite households to seek, discover, and do God's will regarding their financial generosity, then offering a variety of ways for them to give will help connect their heartfelt passion with a *number* of different ways that God is working through the life of the church.

Have you ever noticed that colleges and universities are almost *always* in capital campaigns? Why is that? Perhaps they realize that every single season of the year, there will be alumni or friends of the university who have the financial means to give a gift that they weren't able to give the previous season, and they may not be in a position to give this particular gift in the future. In the blessing of the now, campuses will have a variety of ways for donors to invest in the good work of the university.

Churches can learn from other non-profits who have developed strategies for receiving capital contributions all throughout the year. For your church, the capital needs are evident. The people who love Jesus and love your church want to invest in the work of God, but they need to know what the needs are and be invited to invest in them.

Cultivating Planned (Legacy) Giving

In the church world, planned giving is the least-sought pocket of generosity and, perhaps, the easiest kind of gift to cultivate. Perhaps church leaders struggle with asking donors to make a planned gift because it is a gift, by nature, that is most often given following the death of the donor, and they may feel uncomfortable about that. Perhaps they fear that planned giving will compete with annual or capital giving. Or maybe they are so focused on annual fundraising and an occasional capital appeal that planned giving is just not on the church's radar screen of the funding priorities. Maybe they don't feel equipped to create and articulate a plan for implementing a planned giving strategy.

Of all of the congregations with which I've had the privilege to be in ministry, the vast majority have no plan for seeking legacy gifts. However, for those congregations that do have a planned giving strategy, there is one thing they have in common: at some point in the church's past, a layperson passed away and remembered the church in their will. The church was able to communicate something like, "A legacy gift has been received from the estate of one of our deceased members. Though this person will no longer be with us in body, we will be blessed for eternity by the gift of this person's generosity because it will continue to impact far beyond this person's life on earth."

Church leaders, have you considered
including your church in your will?

What if the cultivation of planned gifts became a part of the all-year generosity narrative of your church? What if every commitment form for an annual or capital campaign included a simple box to check that said, "I would like to learn more about remembering the church in my will"? What if a group of donors in your church formed a Legacy Society made up of people who have committed to support the congregation long after their time on earth is completed?

There are seasons in the rhythm of a calendar year for which the focus on planned gifts can be a natural part of the conversation in your church:

1. **Early spring/Lent season:** Soon after the beginning of the New Year, have a Wills and Bequests information session for those interested in learning more about remembering your church in their will. Per above, if those making an annual gift were able to check the "I would like learn more about remembering the church in my will" box on the commitment form, invite those who did so to be a part of the information meeting. Invite a church member who is a financial planner and/or a denominational foundation representative to present relevant information. Include testimonials from people who have already included a legacy gift in their will. Announce the formation of a Legacy Society that will gather each fall to share in fellowship and hear updates about your church's legacy ministry.

2. **Summer:** Distribute a planned giving newsletter including your church's annual report from the foundation. Include updates on any legacy gifts received, status of the legacy fund, and stories of lives impacted through the legacy contributions. Include Legacy Society testimonials and an invitation for those interested to consider including the church in their will.

3. **Fall:** Host an annual Legacy Luncheon/Dinner for those who have included the church in their will and for those interested in doing so. Invite an inspiring legacy speaker to be a part of the experience.

Church leaders, have you considered including your church in your will? How many of God's people would gladly offer a portion of their estate for the continued work of God through the church that has meant so much to them? Perhaps creating the provision in your will can be a source of inspiration for beginning or growing the legacy ministry of your church.

Cultivating Special (Designated) Giving:

People love to invest in the parts of the church's ministry that align with their heartfelt passion. In a healthy ministry environment, these special gifts provide opportunities for persons to grow in generosity. They also provide an opportunity for the church to create signature mission projects—the three to five projects for which the church is known in the community. Special gifts also provide a means through which the church can partner with local, regional, national, and global organizations that are doing what one church could never do.

As with any pocket of giving, special gifts can be given 24/7/365 as the donor feels compelled to give. From your church's perspective, the active cultivation of special gifts can happen periodically (monthly or quarterly), throughout the year, and can also align with seasons of the year when people tend to have philanthropic hearts and minds (Christmas and Easter).

Here is a suggested rhythm for the cultivation of special gifts:

1. **Periodic special gifts offerings (either monthly or quarterly):** There are signature mission projects, community projects, or denominational initiatives that can become the focus of quarterly or monthly invitations to give. Many church leaders feel that the monthly communion offering appeal gets lost in the narrative, and others find the monthly rhythm helpful. Church leaders, you can discern whether a monthly, quarterly, or other pattern of asking for special gifts is best for your church.

2. **Special gifts aligned with the timing of special projects:** In my years of pastoral ministry, I discovered that the best time to invite people to invest in something, such as drilling a water well in Central America, would be right after showing a video of the most recent well that was drilled there. It may be that the best Sunday to ask for next year's Vacation Bible School scholarship fund is right after this year's VBS. Once the life-changing impact of *any* special ministry is communicated, it is possible to simply say, "Thank you for your generosity that made this possible, and thank you for the gifts that are given today. They will help the life-changing impact of this ministry to continue in the months and years to come!"

3. **Easter Sunday and Christmas Eve—Give it *all* away?** I'm not even sure who started the trend, but I'm grateful for it. I'm referring to the counter-intuitive trend of giving away 100 percent of the Easter Sunday and Christmas Eve offerings to community partners or national and global mission partners. During my first eighteen or so years of pastoring, I recall that Easter Sunday was the highest attended Sunday with a disproportionately low offering. The Christmas Eve offering was

often used to help with the year-end shortfall in annual giving. Then, one year, a couple of months before Christmas Eve, I suggested to our finance team that we identify three community mission partners and divide 100 percent of the Christmas Eve offering equally between the three organizations. The result was mind-blowing—a 300 percent increase in the offering received from the previous Christmas Eve. What was equally surprising is that we finished the year strong that year with annual giving—just like we did every year!

Since it worked on Christmas Eve, we did the same for the Easter Sunday offering, this time highlighting two national/global mission partner organizations. Like Christmas Eve, we highlighted each organization just prior to the offering time, and again, the result was amazing—a 100 percent increase from the previous year's Easter Sunday offering.

How do you think your members and guests would respond to that kind of an invitation? How would your finance team react to the idea of giving away 100 percent of these offerings? It's a leap of faith but one that continues to inspire and amaze me years later. I'm grateful to the vision of an un-named church leader who first said, "Let's give it all away!" Christmas is a time of giving and Easter is a time of resurrection and new life. These two holy seasons are ideal for seeking special gifts that will change lives locally and across the world.

Our Creator made us to be generous.

What will your strategy for all-year generosity be? Hopefully, aligning opportunities for giving with the seasons of the year and the seasons of your particular church's year—as well as some unique opportunities on a couple of high holy days—will help you create an effective plan for your church.

Just to quickly recap, start with one or two ideas mentioned in this chapter, then continue to develop an indigenous generosity calendar for your unique context. As you are able to illustrate the life-changing impact of the work of God through your church—and as you provide opportunities that will multiply your effectiveness—your people will give. Our Creator made us to be generous. If we equip people with the information they need to understand and with the stories that inspire generosity, they will grow in the grace of giving.

CONVERSATION STARTERS
FOR YOUR TEAM

1. In what ways are the four pockets of giving (annual, capital, planned, special) evident in your congregation?

2. Which pocket of giving is strongest, and which is most in need of attention?

3. In revisiting the first paragraph in this chapter, what are two or three suggestions that can be adapted to your church's generosity ministry right now?

REMEMBER THE LEGACY, LEAD WELL, AND SAY THANK YOU AS NEVER BEFORE

REMEMBER THE LEGACY OF GENEROSITY

"Where's Edna? She didn't say anything about being out of town this morning," asked a concerned friend.

"I was wondering the same thing myself," replied equally concerned Pastor Radde.

"It's not like her to miss church. I'll run by and check on her. She may not be feeling well."

Minutes later, Pastor Radde arrived at my Grandma Williams's home. He tried the front door, but there was no answer. He went around the back of the house and peered into the kitchen window. Nothing. Looking into the bedroom window, however, he saw Edna still in bed, so he knocked on the windowpane. No Response. Lifting the unlocked window, he climbed through, and then his intuition was confirmed. She had gone to bed the night before and never woke up.

Many would say my Grandma Williams
was poor. But I tell you, she was the
richest person I've ever known.

What the pastor described to us that day will always be a source of both comfort and inspiration. The transistor radio was still on and tuned to the AM station, so she didn't miss a baseball game of her beloved Texas Rangers. Her Sunday dress was hanging solitarily from the hanger on the closet door. And on the dresser was her signed check already written out to First Methodist Church of Mexia, Texas. The amount of contribution reflected her tithe—a full 10 percent of her meager weekly retirement income paid to widows of Methodist pastors.

Grandma was the spiritual rock of our family. As a young boy, I would sit on her lap, and she would read to me the stories of Jesus. I never heard her utter a negative word about anyone. At her death, she didn't own a car—she never even drove one. She didn't own a house, but the small, retired pastor's parsonage on East Palestine Street was as warm and hospitable as any home I've ever visited. She didn't have fancy clothes or jewelry. And financial resources? She had just enough money for her own funeral arrangements. Many would say my Grandma Williams was poor. But I tell you, she was the richest person I've ever known. And when I think of her legacy of generosity, she is at the top of the list of generous givers.

All of us have people in our lives who have embodied generosity, sacrifice, and unconditional love. Who are some of yours? For me, I'm grateful for Grandma Williams and the host of people in my life who make up my personal "roll call of the faithful."

LEAD PEOPLE ON A JOURNEY
THAT YOU ARE WILLING TO TAKE

As much as generosity was modeled well by my Grandma and others, I have struggled to reflect that legacy in my own journey. Looking back on my twenty years as a lead pastor, I confess that I did not lead well in the area of financial generosity until one day I will always remember— the day a mentor told me the truth. I had preached percentage giving, but my walk didn't match my talk. Over ten years' time, our household giving increased, but not at the same rate my salary had increased. My wife and I were committed to giving a planned percentage for the work of God, but it wasn't a tithe—not even close.

At the time, I was preparing for a fourth capital campaign, which was for a second expansion for a relatively new church, as well as a campaign that would reduce its long-term debt. The church hired a mentor of mine named Michael to facilitate the fundraising, and I was invited to do something I had never done before. Michael asked me to consider sharing with the team what my wife and I would be giving for our three-year household gift—over and above our annual giving—in support of the campaign vision. He asked me to pray about it and get back to him. I confess that I didn't pray about it—I didn't even ask my spouse if she would pray with me about it.

> Church leaders: you cannot lead
> people on a journey that you're
> not willing to take yourself.

Michael's challenge showed me that I was asking everyone else to prayerfully consider sacrificial support, yet I had not even begun to pray myself. One day shortly after, he asked me, "Don, have you determined what your household gift will be for the three-year giving period?" I said yes and then told him the number. There was a long silence. Then Michael spoke words I can recall as if it were yesterday.

"Don, if you don't mind, please don't share that information with anyone. It would not be beneficial to the campaign and may actually harm the campaign."

I thanked Michael for his honesty. Later, instead of sulking or getting angry or defensive, my wife and I started praying. We prayed separately, and we prayed together. Eventually—and amazingly—we both discerned the same number for our three-year household commitment. It was a number that was exponentially higher than the one I initially reported to Michael. Together, when the time was right, Amy and I were able to share with the campaign leadership team the financial commitment we believed God was leading us to make. Not surprisingly, as I reflect on this journey, my fourth campaign as a lead pastor was more fruitful than the total of the three previous campaigns combined.

Church leaders: you cannot lead people on a journey that you're not willing to take yourself.

This leads me to point out:

- If you are committed to telling stories about life change in others, are you prepared to share the impact that God has made in *your* life as well?

- If you invite people to discern how they are going to bring their offerings to church, have you begun the same process of discernment for yourself? Have you openly shared your process and what you are learning and discovering?

- If you invite others to consider giving a recurring gift, then be sure to set up your own recurring gift for the church. Or, if for you, recurring giving means faithfully writing a check each month and bringing it to the church like you've done for decades, then celebrate your clarity on this, and share your journey with others.

- If you encourage your congregation to pray for God's guidance regarding percentage giving, then pray for the leading of the Spirit about your own personal and household journey of generosity.

- If generosity is a journey of gratitude, prayer, and faith, are you on such a path in your own life?

GET TO KNOW YOUR DONORS— ONE CONVERSATION AT A TIME

In the book *The Ministry of Giving: Fund Your Vision by Developing Your Financial Leaders*, one of the authors, Joel Mikell, makes the distinction between the ministry leaders and financial leaders of your church. Think about it. There are those in every congregation who lead by sharing their spiritual gifts and talents in the ministries of the church (ministry leaders). There are also those who lead through their financial generosity (financial leaders), and there are some who are both ministry *and* financial leaders. [27] I believe churches have typically done well in expressing gratitude to ministry leaders but have consistently failed to say thank you to those who, through their financial generosity, are used by God to fund a disproportionately large percentage of the ongoing ministry and mission of the church.

Church leaders naturally say thank you to ministry leaders because they regularly see the work they do and the heart for God that motivates them. Perhaps one reason we often have neglected to express gratitude toward our financial leaders is that we haven't gotten to know them. We haven't taken the time to discover what motivates them to invest generously in the work of God through the church. Many times, pastors don't even know who their financial leaders are because they aren't aware of what anyone gives. This may be a decision that the pastor has made, or a congregation may actually have a policy that prevents the pastor from knowing how much people give. Whatever the reasons for not knowing, there is one thing related to this matter that is true: pastors who don't know who their financial leaders are will not be able to adequately express gratitude.

It is true that ministry leaders offer their time and talents out of a sense of heartfelt passion for what they have been equipped by God to do. Church leaders are able to observe the ways that people serve and the heart out of which they offer their spiritual gifts.

Regarding financial leaders, it's more challenging to know their heart and the passion behind their generosity. This is where, one conversation at a time, church leaders—particularly the senior or lead pastor—can discover more about their financial donors. Financial generosity happens when there is a connection between what the donor wants to happen and what the church wants to happen—when the passion of the donor is in sync with the church's vision for the future. Discovering this point of connection takes time and intentional conversation.

The non-profit fundraising world refers to these ongoing conversations as *gift cultivation*. This brings to mind a friend who is on the development staff of a large university. Years ago, he and I were discussing the differences between working in the university development world versus the financial stewardship world in churches. At that time, the differences were significant, especially regarding the span of time it took to cultivate a large gift. He offered a scenario, where through the cultivation of a relationship with long-time donors, he came to know and appreciate the couple's passion for education. He became aware of their journey through which this passion had grown, as well as their journey of being blessed with the resources they had accumulated through the decades. When the school had a need to renovate a building that provided a good environment for training students wanting to become educators, the developer knew exactly whom to go to because he had already cultivated a relationship with the couple who had the passion and resources to invest. And here's what was shocking to me: It was two years from the time the university's development person first started the conversation to the time he invited the donor to invest. *Two years.* By then, there was absolute clarity regarding the donor's passion and desire, as well as clarity of the school's vision for the future. For me, it was inspiring and humbling to hear my friend describe this journey.

Where colleges and universities have thrived for a very long time, churches have struggled. Most pastors, frankly, are uncomfortable having a conversation about money at all, much less initiating a conversation with generous donors about what motivates them to give sacrificially. But if we truly want to grow a culture of financial generosity, we're going to have to get to know each person's passion. And in order to get to know them, we've got to know where they are on their journey. We need to know more about the things that bring them great joy and the things that make them cry. In the process, we'll be challenged to search our own hearts to discover those things in ourselves.

> It is easy for the challenges to take priority over the cultivation. It is easy for the perceived problems to take precedence over the opportunities.

A pastor friend of mine serves a congregation where there are multiple worship communities on the church's main campus, as well as in other parts of the city. Every year, the lead pastor and the pastor for the modern worship venue look at the list of the church's one hundred largest donors. They divide the list up, and each week throughout the year (on average), each pastor has one conversation either at the church, over lunch at a restaurant, or at the home of the church member. It may seem obvious, but I'll go ahead and say that the two pastors meet wherever the donor feels most comfortable. Together, these two pastors are committed to having one hundred conversations a year. Not surprisingly, some of those conversations lead to follow-up conversations.

The agenda for each of these conversations is simple:

- Say thank you for the ways the donor's financial generosity has made ministry possible.

- Ask, "What's something I don't know about you that you'd like for me to know?"

- Ask, "What one or two things happening at the church right now inspire you or excite you the most?"

- Ask, "What's one dream that you have for our church?"

What's *not* on the agenda for these conversations? Asking the donor for a future gift for an upcoming need of the church. There's a time and place for that, but not in a gratitude conversation. These one hundred conversations are for the primary purpose of saying two important words: *thank you.*

Church leaders have a lot of conversations throughout the week. During my pastor days, I remember so many of these conversations as troubleshooting in nature, and I would often refer to them as "stamping out brushfires." So, keep this in mind: it is easy for the challenges to take priority over the cultivation. It is easy for the perceived problems to take precedence over the opportunities.

Back to the two pastors and their commitment to have one hundred gratitude conversations (fifty per pastor) a year every year. These pastors lead a very large church and are *crazy* busy. When I'm trying to get on one of their calendars, it takes some creative scheduling for us to find just an hour for lunch every six months or so. But every week, these two pastors find a day and a time to spend at least one hour in conversation with the people whom God is using to fund the lion's share of the contributions this church receives every year.

Two pastors—one conversation each per week—two conversations a week for fifty weeks a year. That's a doable strategy for any pastor who's committed to getting to know the financial leaders of the church in order to express gratitude and tap into the heart and passion of what motivates them to give as they do. And from a selfish standpoint, that's doable for any pastor who wants a front-row seat into the minds, hearts, and journeys of the people who have a major role in funding the life-changing ministry of the church. There is much to learn through conversations like these, but it takes disciplined commitment to implement a very simple, effective plan to cultivate these relationships.

Pastors, are you committed to getting to know your donors? If so, then start with a conversation every other week for the first six months. Make scheduling one a priority. Meet at the location most convenient for the person you'd like to get to know better. Keep the agenda simple. Be inspired by the ways that God's Spirit is guiding your donors into living a generous life. And continue to discern what this means for your own journey of generosity.

MEET PEOPLE WHERE THEY ARE AND INVITE THEM ON A JOURNEY OF GENEROSITY

There are many ways to be generous—time, talent, and treasure. The path of building financial generosity is a path worth taking. As church leaders, once we've decided to take that path ourselves, we will likely be inspired to invite others to discover the joy of generosity.

Recently, I began facilitating an annual fundraising process that asks every household in the church to identify where they are in relation to their journey of financial giving. This process was originally developed by Reverend Larry Sykora under a different branding, but is now called "Pathways to Generosity"—a.k.a. P2G. I'm grateful for Larry's vision for equipping congregations to fund the ongoing life-changing ministries of the church.

P2G invites each household to self-identify as one of the following:

- **Exploring Giver**—one who is giving a first-ever recorded contribution: The reality is that, in many churches, between one-third and one-half of all active households have no recorded gifts. Without judgment, shame, or any public acknowledgement, households are simply asked to reflect on the possibility of moving from a place of "no recorded gift" to a place of "readiness to make a gift." This *exploring* step is the first step along the giving path.

- **Growing Giver**—one who is giving a planned percentage of income: The next step along the path is simply one of growing one's giving. In the "Pathways to Generosity" approach, the goal is not to ask a household to change where they are on their giving path. The goal is for the household to identify where they are and then pray a simple prayer, "God where do you want me to be in my giving?" Ultimately, the journey of financial generosity is a journey of seeking, discovering, and doing God's will as each person perceives God's direction.

- **Deepening Giver**—one who is increasing the percentage of income given: As the joy of generosity is experienced, the discernment may lead a donor to invest a greater percentage of income over time.

- **Centering Giver**—one who is tithing: This occurs when the giver takes steps of faith to give 10 percent of household income for the work of God through the church.

- **Transforming Giver**—one who is investing more than 10 percent of income: This extravagant generosity illustrates a response as discerned through a journey of gratitude, prayer, and faith.

One of the reasons I love the "Pathways to Generosity" approach is that at no time does the church say to its people, "It's time for you to give this," or, "We believe that God is calling everyone to give 10 percent of their adjusted gross income," or, "We believe that God is calling everyone to increase their giving by at least two percent during the upcoming annual campaign." Now, I'm very good at what I do, but *I have no idea* what God's will is for the Sanchez family or for Robert Smith or any other household. And even as a pastor, even though I knew the people in my church, I didn't know God's will regarding what financial generosity looked like for the people with whom I was in ministry.

If every household *seeks* God's will,
discovers God's will, and then *does* God's
will regarding their financial giving, then
your church will have the resources it needs
to do what God is calling you to do.

In my opinion, your role as a pastor or finance team leader or lay leader is not to prescribe financial formulas for the people entrusted to your care. I recently heard about a church where, during the fall stewardship emphasis, the pastor invited every household to increase financial giving by one percent. My initial thoughts were, *what about the single parent who just got furloughed?* And *what about the couple whose high school child suffers from addiction and needs an expensive residential treatment?* Conversely, *what about the couple who just got a financial windfall and have the capacity to increase their giving by 100 percent?* Is it God's will for them to increase their giving by only 1 percent? Perhaps it is, but most likely it isn't. Formulaic appeals do not honor the unique circumstances of each household and the unique ways God's Spirit works in every person's life.

So let's create an environment where people are invited to discover the joy of generosity through a season of prayerful discernment. If every household *seeks* God's will, *discovers* God's will, and then *does* God's will regarding their financial giving, then your church will have the resources it needs to do what God is calling you to do. And once people have identified where they are on their giving path, let's meet them there and say thank you in a way that acknowledges, honors, and celebrates their generosity.

OFFER PERSONAL EXPRESSIONS OF GRATITUDE OFTEN

Once we, as church leaders, are on the path of financial generosity ourselves, we will be more authentic in our ability to connect with others who want to take that journey of generosity as well. And once we become aware that there are those who are leading through their financial giving, how will we respond?

The days of donor-obligated giving are long gone. Kristine Miller, the generosity strategist I mentioned earlier who specializes in faith-based charitable fundraising, states that, "For 90 percent of donors, the most effective piece of communication that they receive is a thank-you note." Miller suggests that "because of this, first-time givers are more likely to consider a second gift based on the thank-you they received after the first gift. A simple note of thanks is more important than any other future appeal for giving they may receive."[28]

The data confirms how difficult it is to retain donors who make a first-time contribution to a church. Brent Spicer, executive vice president of MortarStone, which is a church data analytics provider, states that only 20 to 30 percent of a church's first-time donors will continue giving to the church twelve months later.[29] Why? There are multiple factors, but a primary reason for the lack of donor retention is that the church, into whose ministries they gave, never got around to saying two very simple words: *thank you.*

Church leaders, are you intentionally and strategically expressing gratitude to those through whom the financial resources for your congregation's mission are being invested?

Meister Eckhart, thirteenth-century German philosopher, once stated: "If the only prayer you ever said was, 'thank you,' that would suffice." Giving thanks to God is an important part of your journey with your Creator. Likewise, personally saying thank you to those who bless the ministries of your church with their financial generosity is an important part of your role as a church leader. And yet, for some reason, most church leaders fail to build a culture of gratitude for the generosity of the people. Most churches have no clear process in place to say a very simple thank you on a regular basis.

The *Giving* USA data referenced in *Habit 2: Say Hello to Storytelling* provides the sobering reality that, from 1980 to 2019, faith-based nonprofits in America went from receiving fifty-nine cents of every charitable dollar given to twenty-nine cents. A main reason for this decline is that most church leaders do not know their donors. Some may even get offended that I would refer to people as donors. Meanwhile, the remaining 1.3+ million non-profit organizations are getting to know their donors very well and are cultivating relationships in strategic ways.

The results speak for themselves. Church leaders, are you intention-ally and strategically expressing gratitude to those through whom the financial resources for your congregation's mission are being invested?

I've already confessed that I was not generous to the churches I served early in my ministry. I gave more than most, I suppose, but I didn't honestly know who gave what. Perhaps I was so uncomfortable with my own journey of giving, I didn't want to know about anyone else's. I would even say during annual fundraising sermons, "I make it a point *not* to know what people give." I was never taught to say that; I just started saying it and continued to say it at least once a year dur-ing the fall stewardship campaign. In making that declaration, I now believe that I was giving permission to people who were stuck in their own financial journeys to continue to stay stuck.

I look back on that and wonder what I was thinking. In every other area of their existence, I wanted them to live healthy lives. If someone said they didn't know the Bible very well, I would have helped them learn more about the scriptures. If they were physically sick or expe-riencing emotional or relational struggles, I would have tried to assist and support them any way I could. Yet, in the one area that Jesus said was a key indicator of a person's journey of discipleship (the steward-ship of their earthly treasure), I had no interest in knowing who needed help and who needed a special word of thanks. I was not stewarding my own treasure well, and I certainly wasn't helping others discover the joy of financial generosity.

And now, more than thirty years later, I continue to meet pastors who remind me of me back in the day.

Later in ministry, I became more intentional about connecting with donor households. In one instance, I did the math and discovered that, out of 1,200 households in the church, the top one hundred donors were giving more than 60 percent of the total annual income for the mission and ministry of the church. When I realized that about 8 per-cent of households were funding 60 percent of the church's mission,

I felt compelled to personally write one hundred thank-you notes in January to say, "Thank you for your generosity this past year. Through your giving, we had a year like never before!" The reaction was surprising. Several of those to whom I wrote expressed appreciation for the note. A couple of them went on to say that they had never received a note of gratitude from a pastor during all their years of giving.

Over the past forty years, while church leaders have largely failed to connect with their financial leaders and all who give regularly to the work of God through the church, charitable organizations have done their due diligence. The consequence for churches? A 50 percent reduction in their piece of the philanthropic pie.

STRATEGIES FOR SAYING THANK YOU ALL YEAR

In the previous chapter, you considered a plan for growing generosity all year long. Now it's time to include, as a part of the all-year plan, a strategy for how you will actually say thank you throughout the year to those who have generously given.

Within the all-year generosity plan, there are times when expressing gratitude is a natural part of the rhythm. Here are some strategic times to consider. Some are calendar-driven, and others are non-calendar milestones.

Calendar-Driven Milestones

- **In January, (after the close of the calendar year):** In the new year, send letters of gratitude to every household that gave during the past year. These letters should include how money has been invested in life-changing ways, as well as the vision for the coming year. But the main focus is essentially to say, "Thank you. This is how your investment in the work of God through the church has resulted in changed lives." Highlight stories that summarize the kinds of fruitful ministry that is happening within the church, the community, and the world.

- **Quarterly (at the three, six, and nine-month milestones):** The quarterly letters and statements should be segmented based on the following scenarios:

  – Those who made an estimate of giving and are actively giving

  – Those who made an estimate of giving and have not yet given year-to-date

  – Those who did not provide an estimate of giving and have made some recorded financial gift year-to-date

  – Those who did not provide an estimate of giving and have not yet given a recorded gift year-to-date

  – Those who are new to the church since the last quarterly statement

  While these letters will vary based on the segment that best applies to each household, the letter will be consistent in highlighting the ministries that have been supported year-to-date and a ministry vision for the remaining months of the year.

- **The beginning of December:** For the same reason church leaders should distribute a capital improvements wish list toward the end of the year, they should also distribute the year-to-date financial statement through the first eleven months of the year. For households that may have fallen behind in regular giving, and for those who have received a financial windfall in the fourth quarter, the update (including several life-changing stories) will not only offer an invitation to generosity, but there will be several weeks remaining in the year during which they can respond.

- **During the financial commitment season of the church.** If your church has an annual fundraising emphasis through which households are invited to offer an estimate of their financial giving for the coming year, it should also include personalized communication updating each household on their current year-to-date giving.

One of the reasons generosity grows in a church is because the leaders of the church have grown in their own generosity.

Other Non-Calendar Milestones

- **A person/household makes a first-time financial gift.** In the non-profit fundraising world, when a donor makes a first-time gift, that person is wanting to start a conversation. This is why a first-ever contribution is often a "leading indicator" of a donor's desire to become more involved in the life of the organization. In starting the conversation, a first-time donor may be asking questions such as:
  - "What will the church's response be to this gift?"
  - "From whom and how will the acknowledgement of the gift be made?"
  - "How will this gift be invested/stewarded by the church's leaders?"

Does your church have a strategy for saying thank you when someone gives a first-ever recorded gift? If not, you should consider creating one. The likelihood of a second gift will be significantly impacted by the church's response to the first gift. When I gave a first-time gift to Habitat for Humanity and the local food pantry, I received a handwritten thank-you note from the executive directors of both organizations. When I've given first-time gifts to churches, the response has been—more often than not—crickets. There are analytical tools available to help churches create a financial dashboard to help its leaders readily identify things like first-time contributions. See www.tools4church.com and www.mortarstone.com to learn more.

- **A donor gives a significant gift compared to the typical giving pattern of the household.** If the Lopez family ordinarily gives $1,000 a month and suddenly gives $5,000, a simple expression of gratitude is not only appropriate but important. Did I mention simple? "Dear Carlos and Maria, I'm writing to simply thank you for your financial generosity and for all of the ways that you invest yourselves and your resources in the work of God through our church. It is a joy to be in ministry with you. Gratefully, Pastor Sandra."

  When, for whatever reason, a household gives a gift that is clearly above and beyond the typical range of giving, it just makes sense to acknowledge it and say thanks! How will you know when such a gift has been given? There are analytical tools that will notify you when this happens! This is just another way of getting to know the households in your church better (see www.tools4church.com or www.mortarstone.com).

- **A person/household completes a financial commitment.** One of the reasons I did not include this means of expressing gratitude in the calendar-related milestones section is because, when a donor fulfills a financial commitment, the church leaders should have a strategy to acknowledge that and express gratitude right after it happens. This could happen any month during the year, depending on the donor. Many churches wait until the end of the year to thank donors for completing a commitment or pledge. The optimal time to say thank you is whenever the estimated financial giving for the year has been fulfilled! Imagine a donor fulfilling an annual commitment by making a lump sum gift in January. How would it feel if the pastor—or other designated person—waited until the following January to acknowledge their generosity?

● ● ●

It has been a joy and an inspiration to help congregations create a culture of growth in financial generosity. Through the years, I've become fully convinced that one of the reasons generosity grows in a church is because the leaders of the church have grown in their own generosity. When they do, they naturally want to invite others throughout the year to live a more generous life. If you are committed to creating an all-year plan for cultivating increased giving, then you should also create an all-year rhythm of saying thank you to the people who are walking the generosity path with you.

WHO SAYS THANK YOU, AND WHEN

Perhaps you're wondering, *who offers these expressions of gratitude?* This is where I get to give my favorite answer to questions like this, and that is, *it depends.*

Each church is unique, but I will offer my opinion just based on my own season of pastoring as well as church leaders I've observed over the years. From my perspective, there are milestones during the year when there is no substitute for the senior pastor writing the note. Pastors, perhaps you are wondering where you will find the time for this. While I have no idea about your particular schedule, I do know that we find the time for the things in life and ministry that are priorities. I also remember that, when my wife and I attended a church with ten thousand members, we received a handwritten note of gratitude from the senior pastor when we completed our online commitment card for the coming year. NOTE: The handwritten note was *literally* four words long, but it made an impact, and I still remember it!

Here are some considerations regarding the question about who expresses gratitude depending on different situations:

- **Senior Pastor:** There's no substitute for the senior pastor to say thank you in a personal way at least one time a year.

- **Finance Team Leader:** The team leader doesn't need to know what people give, but they can certainly write notes of gratitude to key donors.

- **Strategic Staff:** If a special gift is given to the music ministry, then the music director should express gratitude. If a family with children gives a first-ever gift to the church, the senior pastor can write the first thank-you note. The response to a second gift could be a thank-you note written by the children's ministry director.

Create a plan where key leaders in the church are a part of the culture of expressing gratitude. As your church finds its rhythm and pattern for saying thank you, the growing culture of generosity will be enhanced and supported by the culture of gratitude that emerges as well.

START WITH YOURSELF
AND GO FROM THERE

Generosity is contagious, and it really does begin with you! Church leaders, when you are on the joy-filled journey of generosity, then you will want the people in your spiritual family to grow with you in the grace of giving.

Ultimately, this book began with a simple thought process: the physical offering plate has more than outlived its intended purpose. For many, this has been the case for years! Enter the season of COVID-19, and out of necessity, we stopped passing a physical offering plate during a time of virtual worship. We've survived, and many of our churches have even thrived financially during those days. Is it time, therefore, for you, as church leaders, to at least consider that you never have to pass a physical plate again? In its place, a virtual container for 24/7/365 contributions has been created, and we now find ourselves in the midst of an opportunity to grow generosity in ways we never imagined.

In short, a book about moving beyond plate-passing became a book about growing and inspiring generosity within ourselves and the people in our spiritual family called the church. I hope that, through this book, you have been given tools to continue to lead the church in an ever-changing world.

Through considering the five unmistakable habits, you *can* inspire the generosity needed to fund the mission and ministry of your church. A season of discerning and implementing these practices can result in a better offering than ever before, as the people of your church offer their financial gifts, and yes, their *whole lives* to the work of God among you.

And you don't need to pass an offering plate to do it.

CONVERSATION STARTERS
FOR YOUR TEAM

1. This chapter invites you, as church leaders, to consider your individual stewardship journeys. In what ways are you leading by example, and in what ways do you still need to grow in your own journey of generosity?

2. When you think about the people in your church, what are some ways that you would express gratitude to God for their generosity?

3. Discuss the ways you currently express gratitude to your financial donors. What two suggested practices for saying thank you can you immediately begin to implement at your church?

THE HOW-TO GUIDE FOR STORYTELLING IN WORSHIP: A VALUABLE, PRACTICAL RESOURCE

YOU HAVE A UNIQUE STORY FOR MISSION AND MINISTRY—TELL IT!

Each congregation is unique—its history, its context, its people, its ministries. Each church body has a non-transferable mission to which God has called it and is like no other congregation ever. Consider this: God has equipped your church to do what no other congregation can do exactly the way you can! Based on the collective giftedness of the people—or the size and location—God can use your congregation to reach certain kinds of people in ways that no other congregation is equipped to do.

Your church is one-of-a-kind! The *unique story* of your church—and your stories of the work of God within it—are worth telling! Having said that, I invite you to think about these questions:

Do your people know the story of your church? Are they aware of the life-changing work of God that happens throughout each week? Are they able to connect those stories with the collective financial generosity of the people who have found a spiritual home in this unique community of faith? And finally, do your people know what difference God is making in the world through your congregation?

> For the church, the ROI is a life that has been changed for the better.

Through the years, I have partnered in ministry with hundreds of congregations and their leaders. While planting new churches, revitalizing declining churches, funding annual ministry, raising capital funds, promoting legacy giving, and encouraging special giving, I am increasingly inspired by the privilege of being in ministry with each pastor and church leader. Each church has its own unique way through which God is working by changing lives and communities and even the world for the better. Yet I have a sense that most people who say, "That's my church!" do not fully understand the life-changing impact that is happening through the collective financial generosity of members, guests, and friends.

With these hundreds of congregations that I've worked with, and with the thousands of repetitions that our company has had with churches all over the country, I have developed a pretty simple formula for increasing generosity:

Understanding + Ownership + Inspiration = Generosity!

Understanding is a critical part of the generosity equation. Think about it: I'm not going to give at my full financial capacity if I don't fully understand what it is I'm being invited to invest in. Maybe I should have more blind faith, but I'm inclined to want to know what the return on investment (ROI) is. And for the church, the ROI is a life that has been changed for the better. Perhaps my grandparents would have given generously to a vague or intangible cause out of uninformed trust. But I want to know more—I want to see tangible results. Most people in the modern world want to know where their money goes and how it's being stewarded.

Tell me nothing about what my church is up to, and I'll still give because I love its people, I believe in the message, and because God instructs me to give. However, tell me something to help me understand more clearly what the ministry impact is, and I'll invest more. In other words, if I fully comprehend the life-change that is going to happen through what's being funded *(understanding)*, and if I feel as though I'm a part of the story *(ownership)* of life-change that has happened and will continue to happen through my generosity, and if I believe that God's Spirit *(inspiration)* is at work in the midst of this ministry or mission, then I will be compelled to give what my Creator leads me to give to support the good work that God is doing through my generous investment. And the best way to provide understanding, ownership, and inspiration is through storytelling.

Storytelling helps to clarify all parts of the generosity formula. Just telling a brief story (and I'm talking about a one- to two-minute story during the weekly worship experience for fifty-two weeks a year) will help people grow in *understanding* the nature of the ministry that is being funded. Ideally, whenever a story is told, the listener will connect emotionally with another person in the vital ministry being highlighted that day. A story will also instill a sense of *ownership* in the work of God that is already happening and will continue to happen through their generous giving. When hearing a story, each individual who has given in some way will think, *I'm a part of that!* Then, as God works in and through the lives of those engaged in the story's narrative, the *inspiration* of the Spirit's work will guide their personal convictions for how they will continue to invest financially. And for those who have never discovered the joy of financial generosity, the story just may be the inspiration of the Spirit they need to joyfully and sacrificially give for the first time. The result? Generosity!

THE HOW-TO GUIDE FOR STORYTELLING IN WORSHIP

This resource is intended to provide a framework for planning and implementing the weekly messaging needed to grow generosity through growing people's sense of understanding, ownership, and inspiration in the work of God through your church. *Do not assume even for one week* that your congregation already knows the stories of life-change that God is doing! Every week, every story makes a difference.

Now, you might be thinking, *okay, Don, I get it, but how do I plan which ones to tell on which Sunday?*

Here's a resource I've created to help. It's called *The How-To Guide for Storytelling in Worship* and includes the following components:

1. Things to consider before creating a plan for weekly storytelling

2. E-chart for mapping out stories to feature

3. Potential pitfalls and ways to ensure a lasting impact of your storytelling plan in weekly worship

You can download *The How-To Guide for Storytelling in Worship* for free at

WWW.ABETTEROFFERING.COM

I encourage you to celebrate your stories by *telling* them. From personal experience, through pastoring and supporting pastors and church leaders, I can say that planning and implementing this strategy will result in a better, more fruitful offering.

ENDNOTES

1. Tod Bolsinger, *Canoeing the Mountains: Christian Leadership in Uncharted Territory*, (Downers Grove, IL: InterVarsity Press, 2015), 27.

2. Andy Odom (Senior Pastor, Canyon Creek Presbyterian Church, Richardson, TX), in a Zoom Conversation, June 2020.

3. Henry Cloud, *Necessary Endings: The Employees, Businesses, and Relationships That All of Us Have to Give Up in Order to Move Forward*, (Nashville, TN: Harper Business, 2011).

4. Ben Stroup, Velocity Strategy Solutions, www.velocitystrategysolutions.com, in a Zoom conversation, October 2020.

5. Ibid.

6. David King, *COVID-19 Congregational Study*, (Indianapolis, IN: Indiana University Lilly Family School of Philanthropy, Lake Institute on Faith and Giving, September 2020), https://scholar works.iupui.edu/bitstream/handle/1805/23791/lake-covid-report2020-2.pdf.

7. The Temple Treasury: The Court of the Women in the Temple, *Bible History*, https://www.bible-history.com/court-of-women/.

8. David C. Norrington, "Fund-Raising: The Methods Used in the Early Church Compared with Those Used in English Churches Today," *Evangelical Quarterly* 70, no.2, (1998).

9. Frank Viola and George Barna, *Pagan Christianity*, (Carol Stream, IL: Tyndale Momentum, 2008).

10. Mark Rogers, "Passing the Plate," *Christianity Today*, March 2019, https://www.christianitytoday.com/history/2009/march/passing-plate.html.

11. Rev. Ken Sloane, (Director of Stewardship and Generosity, Discipleship Ministries), *A Closer Look at the Offering* webinar, September 2020.

12. John Wesley, "Give All You Can," Wesley Center Online, http://wesley.nnu.edu/john-wesley/the-sermons-of-john-wesley-1872-edition/sermon-50-the-use-of-money/.

13. Travis Garner, (Founding Pastor, The Village Church, Nashville, TN), in an interview, August 2020.

14. J. Clif Christopher, *Not Your Parents' Offering Plate: A New Vision for Financial Stewardship*, (Nashville, TN: Abingdon Press, 2008), 2nd ed. (2015).

15. "Giving USA 2020: The Annual Report on Philanthropy for the Year 2019," The Giving Institute, https://www.givinginstitute.org/page/GivingUSA.

16. Jacob Armstrong and Dan Lins, (Founding Pastor and Director of Operations, Providence Church, Mount Juliet, TN), in a Zoom conversation, August 2020.

17. Shankar Vedantam, "Hidden Brain: Creating God," *National Public Radio*, July 2018, https://www.npr.org/2018/07/16/628792048/creating-god.

18. Gil Rendle and Alice Mann, *Holy Conversations: Strategic Planning as Spiritual Practice for Congregations*, (Lanham, MD: Rowman & Littlefield Publishers, 2003).

19. John Thornburg, *Holy Conversation: The "Hard" Is What Makes It Great*, (Austin, TX: Texas Methodist Foundation, 2014), revised 2020 and re-titled, *Life After COVID-19: The Crucial Need for Discernment When We Return*, https://www.virtual-church.org/embracing-a-new-future/life-after-covid-19.

20. Gil Rendle and Alice Mann, *Holy Conversations: Strategic Planning as Spiritual Practice for Congregations*, (Lanham, MD: Rowman & Littlefield Publishers, 2003).

21. Jacob Armstrong and Dan Lins, (Founding Pastor and Director of Operations, Providence Church, Mount Juliet, TN), in a Zoom conversation, August 2020.

22. Vanco Payment Solutions, https://www.vancopayments.com/egiving/churchgoer-giving-study, Churchgoer Giving Study, December 2017.

23. Kirk Dearman, *We Bring the Sacrifice of Praise*, New Spring, Admin. by Brentwood-Benson Music Publishing, Inc., 1984.

24. Lisa and Michael Gungor, *Beautiful Things*, Brash Music, Atlanta, GA, 2010.

25. Matt Gaston, (Senior Pastor, First United Methodist Church, Plano, TX), in a sermon delivered, September 2020.

26. Kristine Miller and Scott McKenzie, *Bounty: Ten Ways to Increase Giving at Your Church.* (Nashville, TN: Abingdon Press, 2013).

27. Joel Mikell, Bill McMillan, and Kimberly Stewart, *The Ministry of Giving: Fund Your Vision by Developing Your Financial Leaders,* (CreateSpace Independent Publishing Platform, 2013).

28. Kristine Miller, Partner, Horizons Stewardship, in a training for the Horizons Team, September 2020.

29. Brent Spicer, Executive Vice President, Mortarstone (see www.mortarstone.com), in a Zoom presentation to the Horizons Team, September 2020.

Made in the USA
Middletown, DE
03 June 2021